S0-CFY-145

JOURNAL · OF
M · O · R · A · L
THEOLOGY

VOLUME 6, NUMBER 1

JANUARY 2017

POPULORUM PROGRESSIO: 50 YEARS

Edited by Mari Rapela Heidt
and Matthew A. Shadle

J O U R N A L · O F
M · O · R · A · L
T H E O L O G Y

Journal of Moral Theology is published semiannually, with issues in January and June. Our mission is to publish scholarly articles in the field of Catholic moral theology, as well as theological treatments of related topics in philosophy, economics, political philosophy, and psychology.

Articles published in the *Journal of Moral Theology* undergo at least two double blind peer reviews. Authors are asked to submit articles electronically to jmt@msmary.edu. Submissions should be prepared for blind review. Microsoft Word format preferred. The editors assume that submissions are not being simultaneously considered for publication in another venue.

Journal of Moral Theology is indexed in the ATLA Catholic Periodical and Literature Index® (CPLI®), a product of the American Theological Library Association. Email: atla@atla.com, www: http://www.atla.com.

ISSN 2166-2851 (print)
ISSN 2166-2118 (online)

Journal of Moral Theology is published by Mount St. Mary's University, 16300 Old Emmitsburg Road, Emmitsburg, MD 21727.

Copyright © 2016 individual authors and Mount St. Mary's University. All rights reserved.

Except for brief quotations in critical publications or reviews, no part of this book may be reproduced in any manner without prior written permission from the publisher. Write: Permissions. Wipf and Stock Publishers, 199 W. 8th Ave., Suite 3, Eugene, OR 97401.

Pickwick Publications, An Imprint of Wipf and Stock Publishers, 199 W. 8th Ave., Suite 3, Eugene, OR 97401. www.wipfandstock.com. ISBN 13: 978-1-5326-1796-6

JOURNAL OF MORAL THEOLOGY

VOLUME 6, NUMBER 1

JANUARY 2017

CONTENTS

JOURNAL · OF
M · O · R · A · L
THEOLOGY

EDITOR
Jason King, *St. Vincent College*

ASSOCIATE EDITOR
David Matzko McCarthy, *Mount St. Mary's University*

MANAGING EDITOR
Kathy Criasia, *Mount St. Mary's University*

EDITORIAL BOARD
Melanie Barrett, *University of St. Mary
of the Lake/Mundelein Seminary*
Jana M. Bennett, *University of Dayton*
Mara Brecht, *St. Norbert College*
Meghan Clark, *St. John's University*
David Cloutier, *The Catholic University of America*
Christopher Denny, *St. John's University*
John J. Fitzgerald, *St. John's University*
Mari Rapela Heidt, *Waukesha, Wisconsin*
Kelly Johnson, *University of Dayton*
Warren Kinghorn, *Duke University*
Kent Lasnoski, *Quincy University*
Ramon Luzarraga, *Benedictine University, Mesa*
M. Therese Lysaught, *Loyola University Chicago*
Paul Christopher Manuel, *American University*
William C. Mattison III, *University of Notre Dame*
Christopher McMahon, *St. Vincent College*
Rev. Daniel Mindling, O.F.M. Cap., *Mount St. Mary's Seminary*
Joel Shuman, *Kings College*
Matthew Shadle, *Marymount University*
Msgr. Stuart Swetland, *Donnelly College*
Christopher P. Vogt, *St. John's University*
Brian Volck, *University of Cincinnati College of Medicine*
Paul Wadell, *St. Norbert College*
Greg Zuschlag, *Oblate School of Theology*

Journal of Moral Theology, Vol. 6, No. 1 (2017): 1-20

Development, Nations, and "The Signs of the Times:" the Historical Context of *Populorum Progressio*

Mari Rapela Heidt

O N EASTER SUNDAY, MARCH 26, 1967, Pope Paul VI issued the encyclical *Populorum Progressio (On the Development of Peoples)*. It was his fourth encyclical in three years and was met with mixed reactions. In some sectors it was lauded as "a document of extraordinary social vision and daring,"[1] "an encyclical that will probably be remembered more than *Mater et Magistra*,"[2] and "unquestionably a major document, committing the resources of the church to the eradication of poverty and bestowing its blessing on secular initiatives toward the same goal."[3] The same commentator also noted, "It is a moving appeal, not only to Catholics but to all men, to regard the socio-economic development of poor countries both as a moral duty and as an essential condition of world peace."[4]

Others found it confusing and too different from prior magisterial documents to offer any kind of direction to the faithful. The *Wall Street Journal* very famously called the encyclical "warmed-over Marxism,"[5] and even seasoned Catholic commentators found themselves at a loss in understanding the new encyclical. Although prior encyclicals also focused on some of the same aspects of economics as *Populorum Progressio*, none addressed the perceived problems in as technical and detailed a manner. *Populorum Progressio* also included no calls to specific faith actions such as evangelization or prayer, except in a very general way, a characteristic it shared with the social encyclicals of John XXIII. Many people felt as René Laurentin did when he wrote in the "Introduction" to *Liberation, Development, and Salvation* that, "I am not an economist and I felt overwhelmed by economics, this basic aspect of the problem."[6] There is also the critique offered by Joseph Martino, that the subject of the encyclical is a result

---

[1] "*Populorum progressio*," *Christian Century*, April 12, 1967, 460.
[2] Colin Clark, "The Development of Peoples, Some Implications of the Papal Encyclical," *The Tablet*, April 15, 1967, 400.
[3] Benjamin L. Masse, "The Pope's Plea for Poor Nations," *America*, August 5, 1967, 129.
[4] Masse, "Pope's Plea," 129.
[5] "A Blessing for Secular Error," *Wall Street Journal*, March 30, 1967, 14A.
[6] René Laurentin, *Liberation, Development, and Salvation*, trans. C.U. Quinn (New York: Orbis Books, 1972), 3.

of "the intellectual fads of the [19]50s and [19]60s."[7] In that era, there was a great deal of concern about development, and the United Nations made development in poor countries the focus of special attention. Of that time, Barbara Ward writes,

> When we look back to the 1960s, we can see most of us caught up in the euphoria of economic growth. It seemed clear that, thanks to the Keynesian revolution of demand management, developed societies had virtually solved their problems. We would gallop forward to the society of high consumption, there to enjoy its felicities—whatever they might prove to be. At the same time, behind us would follow the developing world by 'stages of growth' and the wealth created in the process would inevitably trickle down until it reached the poorest.[8]

In light of these reactions and the inescapable reality of the social and political contexts in which it is embedded, it is possible to see *Populorum Progressio* as a document responding to a particular time, without real enduring value.

And yet, *Populorum Progressio* not only endures but has become the basis of much of contemporary Catholic social teaching, particularly in the areas of economics and economic development, but also international relations, international aid, and the ethics of globalization. It has been commemorated twice by succeeding popes in laudatory encyclicals which both reaffirm and expand the ideas set forth in *Populorum Progressio*: *Sollicitudo Rei Socialis* by John Paul II in 1987 and *Caritas in Veritate* by Benedict XVI in 2009. Most recently, Pope Francis's encyclical *Laudato Si'* embraced the spirit and the language of *Populorum Progressio* in its discussion of the obligation to care for creation, quoting from the initial document and from both of the follow-up encyclicals multiple times. The concepts of the encyclical, particularly its central theme of integral human development, have become even more relevant and prominent in the 50 years since its publication, even when not coupled to economics.

In spite of its importance and the ongoing relevance of the themes of the encyclical, the scholarship on *Populorum Progressio* is remarkably thin. After initial attention in the 1960s, publications discussing the encyclical dropped sharply and have not recovered, except for the

---

[7] Joseph P. Martino, "*Populorum Progressio*: Moral and Economic Implications," *This World*, Summer, 1987, 52.

[8] Barbara Ward, "Looking Back on Populorum Progressio," *Readings in Moral Theology, No. 5: Official Catholic Social Teaching*, eds. Charles E. Curran and Richard A. McCormick (New York: Paulist Press, 1986), 130. For a description of these "stages of growth," see Walter W. Rostow, *The Stages of Economic Growth: A Non-Communist Manifesto* (Cambridge: Cambridge University Press, 1961).

few articles marking anniversaries and the obligatory mentions upon the publications of the commemorative encyclicals. Few serious discussions of the encyclical exist outside of various compendia of Catholic social teaching, and those which do attempt to dissect and understand the document are often published in languages other than English, with translations generally unavailable. The reasons for this lack of resources are unclear, but it presents an impediment to a deeper understanding of the document, particularly in a North American context. A similar but somewhat larger hole exists in analysis of the work of the principal author of *Populorum Progressio,* the French economist Louis-Joseph Lebret. Again, this lack of resources presents a tall challenge, one that has yet to be bridged.

The goal of this essay is to fill in some of the gaps by looking at the historical context of the document, especially the work of its principal author. To do this, I first look at some of the secular historical context of the 1960s which gave rise to the idea of the encyclical, and then move to a brief examination of the work of Louis-Joseph Lebret. As Lebret's work is married to the more philosophical work of Jacques Maritain in the encyclical, a short review of Maritain's work follows. The essay concludes with some suggestions for future investigations.

HISTORICAL BACKGROUND

Populorum Progressio was published in 1967, towards the end of a decade of serious social and ecclesial changes, just prior to the unanticipated upheavals that 1968 and later years would bring to both the world and the church. The document emerged as a part of a long tradition within Catholicism of confronting social and economic problems and proposing solutions that are consonant with the evolving Catholic views of the proper place of economics and economic life within the lives of human beings and societies. It was also, at least in part, a response to the aforementioned social and political realities that emerged in the 1950s and 60s, a time of geopolitical unrest and serious change that enriched some societies while plunging others into poverty and destitution.

Paul VI himself acknowledges the impact of social conditions on his writing, noting at the beginning of *Populorum Progressio* (no. 4) that he was inspired to write the encyclical by his own observations of poverty and the problems brought about by development on trips to Latin America, Africa, the Middle East, and India in the early 1960s. He also was strongly influenced by works that detailed the problems of emerging nations, especially the problems of hunger and poverty wrought by inequalities in economic development. Among these works were *Dynamique concrète du développement*, written by the French Dominican Lebret and detailing economic development problems and their effects in several nations, along with Maritain's *Integral*

Humanism and *Wirtschaft und Gesellschaft* by Oswald von Nell-Breuning.[9]

It is difficult to overstate how much the Cold War dominated and influenced world events in the years leading up to the publication of *Populorum Progressio*, and its echoes can be seen throughout the document (and indeed in previous documents, especially 1963's *Pacem in Terris*). The issues divided much of the world politically into two blocs, with the Soviet Union leading the communist East and the United States at the forefront of the democratic West. The Cold War was not just a war of words, though the rhetoric on both sides was incendiary, nor did the struggle between East and West only manifest itself in ideological debates. Any possibility of "peaceful coexistence" between the superpowers was fragile at best, as evidenced by an ongoing race to develop ever more powerful and destructive weapons. The Atomic Test Ban Treaty of 1963 slowed open-air tests of nuclear weapons but did not slow the development or production of these weapons on either side.

In addition to its conflicts with the West, the Soviet Union faced challenges within communism, as evidenced by a struggle with China over who would lead the communist world. The mid-1960s saw the beginnings of another communist bloc, as the Chinese attempted to extend their influence over emerging nations in Asia and Africa. China faced its own problems with the Nationalist Chinese, who held the island of Formosa (now known as the nation of Taiwan) along with a seat in the United Nations. (Mainland China did not gain its own seat in the UN until a compromise was reached in the 1970s.)

In addition to conflicts between the superpowers, wars and unrest dominated large parts of the world in this period. Pakistan and India were at war over the area known as Kashmir, territory that was claimed by both sides. A peace agreement was reached on this issue shortly before the publication of *Populorum Progressio*. Israel had several military conflicts with its neighbors Syria and Jordan, with each side claiming justification because of prior antagonism by the other. Conflicts like these eventually escalated into war in 1967. In Southeast Asia, the United States became embroiled in a civil war in Vietnam, which escalated sharply throughout the composition of the encyclical, reaching a high point in terms of combat deaths the year after its publication. Political unrest was also widespread in Europe as Charles de Gaulle threatened to withdraw France from NATO and from the European Economic Community while long-established political alliances were overturned or tested in other countries, often resulting in new leaders coming to power.

---

[9] Giorgio Campanini, "*Le Radici Culturali del Nuovo Umanesimo Proposto dalla 'Populorum Progressio,'*" in *Il Magistero di Paolo VI nell' enciclica Populorum Progressio* (Brescia: Istituto Paolo VI; Rome: Edizioni Studium, 1989), 43.

As overriding a factor as the Cold War was in shaping world events in the 1960s, it was the continuing effects of decolonization and on-going struggles for independence by colonies that likely had a greater role in shaping *Populorum Progressio*. Throughout the late 1950s and into the 1960s, many of the countries of Asia and almost the entire continent of Africa became independent of the countries which had claimed and colonized them, most notably France, Britain, and Belgium. Nations as diverse as Vietnam and Indonesia in Asia, Southern Yemen (later the reunified Republic of Yemen) and Lebanon in the Middle East, and most of the African continent emerged from colonial rule. If one includes the total populations of these colonial nations and the populations of the colonizers, the process of decolonization affected more than one billion people, one third of the total world population at the time. Like the Cold War, it is difficult to overstate the effects of this decolonization on the whole of the world population. In many ways, these former colonies still feel the effects of decolonization. The emergence of so many new nations at one time would not occur again until the fall of communism and the dissolution of the Soviet Union and its satellite states in the early to mid-1990s.

Conditions in these former colonies were not always good or conducive to prosperity. Along with wars for independence that destroyed lives and used up resources and the struggles of newly-formed nations to learn to govern themselves and to establish economies that could meet the needs of their people without the support of the colonial powers came a great deal of instability within those regions, leading to a general sense of instability throughout the world. On the continent of Africa in particular, there were many conflicts concerning the borders of the new nations and many shifts in those borders before the countries stabilized and became independent states. Wars between various factions for control of the new nations were common, and some civil wars drew the involvement of larger states. The civil war in Congo (later Zaire), for example, drew the involvement of both the United States and France. *Coups d'état* were common, and military regimes were prevalent throughout Africa, often replacing elected governments through violence. In addition, those new governments also had ideological struggles, as the United States, the Soviets, and the Chinese all attempted to influence the political cultures of emerging nations.

Some countries in Africa faced challenges of a different kind, as both Rhodesia (now Zimbabwe) and South Africa, both former British colonies, imposed white minority rule on the black majority, with South Africa going further by imposing a system of racial segregation, called apartheid, on the country. Rhodesia eliminated white minority rule and became the independent state of Zimbabwe in 1980, and South Africa's system of apartheid finally collapsed in 1991, though challenges remain in these countries and throughout states which had

embraced political systems that reflected those of their former colonizers.

As rapidly as things were changing in a geo-political sense, they
were also changing within Catholicism. Paul VI became pope in the
midst of the Second Vatican Council, a council he allowed to continue
after the death of his predecessor, John XXIII. By 1967, the work of
the Council was finished, and the long work of implementing the
changes wrought by the council was really just beginning, an arduous
process that could still be considered somewhat unfinished 50 years
later. In addition to the council, the pope was under some pressure to
issue guidance on the use of artificial birth control, a question which
had been under consideration for years and would not be resolved for
more than another year.

COMPOSITION AND INFLUENCES

Populorum Progressio was a document long in the making. Work
on the encyclical began late in 1963, the first year of Paul's papacy,
when he asked Lebret for a preparatory summary on development that
would serve as the basis for a new encyclical.[10] Paul VI had long ad-
mired Lebret's work and had hoped that some aspects of what would
become *Populorum Progressio* would have been a part of *Gaudium et
Spes*. Although *Gaudium et Spes* discussed development, Paul felt the
need for a longer and deeper discussion, one which included some de-
nunciation of the atheistic humanism he saw spreading throughout Europe and with which he had become very concerned as Archbishop of
Milan.[11]

The encyclical went through seven drafts, the first of which was
completed in September of 1964. The first several drafts were written
in French by Lebret, with editing and composition suggestions by
Paul. After Lebret's death in 1966, the final drafts of the encyclical
were completed by Paul Poupard, a French priest who worked in the
Secretariat of State. The final draft of February 16, 1967 was returned
marked "*Sta tutto bene*" ("it's all good") by the Pope, and the encyclical was promulgated on Easter Sunday, March 26, 1967.[12] Before
giving the traditional papal blessing to the city and the world that day,
Paul VI announced his new encyclical, "It seems to us that the proper
time has come, after the recent ecumenical council, to add another

---

[10] François Malley, O.P, *Le Pere Lebret, L'Économie au Service des Hommes* (Paris:
Editions du Cerf, 1968), 99.

[11] Laurentin, *Liberation*, 109.

[12] Marvin L. Krier Mich, *Catholic Social Teaching and Movements* (Connecticut:
Twenty-Third Publications, 1998), 156.

chapter to the teaching on the questions that trouble, torment and divide men in their search for bread, for peace, for freedom, for justice, and for brotherhood."[13]

Beyond his desire to alleviate the suffering of the poor, Paul VI expressed four principal motivations for writing *Populorum Progressio*. First, he wanted to emphasize the theme of development in a stronger way than the Second Vatican Council had, "to approach it in language more direct, more dynamic, and more communicative."[14] While *Gaudium et Spes* dealt with the issue of development, it was a compromise document written by committee, and Paul VI wanted a document that used stronger and more vigorous language than the Council had, one that went beyond the Council's general proposals to issues that were more concrete.

Second, the pope recognized that most of the members of the Council had been from developed, or industrialized, countries and that those countries which were underdeveloped had been under-represented, their voices heard only secondarily. Paul VI wished to stress his concern for the undeveloped and underdeveloped nations of the world and, in a real way, positioned himself as their representative through his document.

A third motivation for Pope Paul VI is mentioned in the text of the encyclical. In no. 4, the pope refers to two trips that he had taken to Latin America in 1960 and to Africa in 1962 which "brought us into direct contact with the acute problems pressing on continents full of life and hope." This paragraph also notes two trips he took after becoming pope, to India and the Holy Land, where he was "able to see and virtually touch the very serious difficulties besetting peoples of long-standing civilizations who are at grips with the problem of development." In *Populorum Progressio*, the pope continues to denounce injustices he witnessed on these trips and, indeed, the inequities in social and cultural progress that he had witnessed since becoming Archbishop of Milan. Finally, Paul's own reflection on the problems of development had led him to make a connection between development and peace, and he wished to express this connection in his encyclical. This led to probably the most famous pronouncement of the encyclical, "development is the new name for peace" (no. 86). René Laurentin, in a work written in response to the Medellín Conference which draws heavily from *Populorum Progressio*, notes that Paul VI had made statements similar to this at least twice before, once in a letter to United Nations Secretary General U Thant in May of 1966, and publicly later that year in a Mass in St. Peter's Square in October.[15]

Populorum Progressio is something of a departure from the social

---

[13] "Drafted in French," *The Tablet*, April 1, 1967, 359.
[14] Laurentin, *Liberation,* 109.
[15] Laurentin, *Liberation*, 109-112.

encyclical tradition, in that it addresses social problems not just from a practical perspective—what should be done?—but goes beyond scriptural themes and natural law argumentation by drawing on modern philosophical and theological movements. The influences of two French intellectuals on its composition, priest-economist Louis-Joseph Lebret and two of his works, *Le drame du siècle* and *Dynamique concrète du développement,* and Catholic political philosopher Jacques Maritain and his work *Humanisme intégral, problèmes temporels et spirituels d'une nouvelle chrétienté,* bear close scrutiny.

LOUIS-JOSEPH LEBRET

By far the greatest influence on the thinking of Paul VI and the actual composition of *Populorum Progressio* is the work of Louis-Joseph Lebret (1897-1966), whose two most important works form the basis for *Populorum Progressio.* Lebret wrote most of the first drafts of the encyclical before his death in 1966, drawing heavily from his own work and even quoting from his prior books verbatim. Lebret's primary concern was economic development and its effects on the poor, not just on living conditions, but also on what might be termed their "spiritual condition."

Lebret was a French Dominican priest who began considering and studying economics and its effects on people during the depressed economy of the 1930s. Lebret came to the priesthood and to economics somewhat later in life than was usual at the time, not entering study for the priesthood until he was 26. Prior to his ordination, he attended the French Naval Academy and served as an officer in the French navy. He was seriously wounded in the First World War. After the war, Lebret served as an instructor for a brief time at the Naval school, teaching maneuvering and navigation skills to navigators and helmsmen. During 1921 and 1922, he was assigned a tour of duty that would profoundly affect him and effectively put an end to his naval career: he served as an envoy and director of movement at the port of Beirut, Lebanon. Lebanon was a French protectorate at that point, and Beirut had been named its capital only in 1920. Lebret's primary duty was to help re-establish Beirut as a functional Middle Eastern port for French ships.

His time in Beirut was Lebret's first experience of real economic hardship and also his first experience with non-Frenchmen. He worked closely with Lebanese citizens and also established a close relationship with a group of Jesuit priests who worked to help rebuild the city. Lebret was recalled from Lebanon late in 1922. He was promoted, made a member of the French Legion of Honor,[16] and received

---

[16] Most French naval officers were made members of the Legion of Honor after the war, see Malley, *Pere Lebret,* 22.

command of a ship, which he accepted. After a few months in command, however, and with his naval career on a fast track, Lebret left the Navy and entered the Dominican novitiate of Lyon in 1923, at Rijckholt, Holland, where the Lyon Dominicans had established a house after their expulsion from France early in the 20th century. He was ordained there in 1930 at the age of 33.

Over the course of nine years, from shortly after his ordination in 1930 until he was recalled into the Navy during the Second World War, Lebret developed the basic method he would use later in life when confronting the economic problems within a society. The first step was to observe the conditions already present and to document them. The second step was to try to understand the causes of these problems and to make a judgment about an appropriate solution to the problems. The last step was action, concrete actions which were designed to solve or alleviate the problems he had observed. Prayer was an important part of action, but concrete material actions to alleviate suffering were also important.

In 1939, when Lebret was recalled to naval service for the Second World War, he served his time as a naval chaplain. In 1941 he settled in a community of Dominicans near Marseilles, where he established a study and research center which he called *Économie et Humanisme*. Originally conceived as a center for the study of Marxism and other economic alternatives, *Économie et Humanisme* evolved into a center for the study of all aspects of the economy and of possible solutions to economic problems that would serve the common good.[17]

The stated goals of *Économie et Humanisme* were inquiry and study, discussion among people of various professions, and the determination of the common good. In this period, Lebret began to write both books and an intermittent periodical published by the center, also called *Économie et Humanisme*. He began to travel widely to study economic conditions in countries beyond France, mostly in French colonies or former French colonies, though he also traveled widely in South America and Francophone areas of Africa and Asia, especially Vietnam. His travels allowed Lebret to refine and sharpen his economic views, which would later open many more doors for him. He was struck by how much economic development within a country affected the people within that country and how uneven development affected the people unevenly. For example, Lebret made his first trip to Brazil in 1947, where he taught a short course in political science in São Paulo. He noted the diversity of development within the city, with a vast gulf between the rich in one part of the city and the poor in another part. The same was true throughout the country: the provinces to the south and west were more prosperous and the people in them richer and healthier, while the provinces to the north and east were

---

[17] Malley, *Pere Lebret*, 58.

poorer and sicker. Lebret noted the same phenomenon in other countries and began to focus on development and developmental problems as a deeper course of study. As early as 1952, Lebret was persuaded that unequal development would be the problem of the century.[18]

In 1956, Lebret passed the day-to-day direction of *Économie et Humanisme* to another so that he could concentrate solely on problems of development and the implications of development. From 1953-56, Lebret served as an expert at a United Nations conference on development. He later became a member of the United Nations' Food and Agriculture Organization and would go on to serve as an economic advisor to the French government and the governments of several emerging nations. His desire to study development, and especially underdeveloped nations, led to the establishment of another research center, the *Institut de Recherches et de formation pour le développement harmonisé* (l'IRFED) in Paris. L'IRFED had a tri-fold purpose: 1) to study development worldwide and to research ways of ensuring a harmonious, or equally distributed, development, 2) the religious formation of participants and those in countries under study, and 3) worldwide travel to observe the conditions of development. Lebret became the general director of l'IRFED.

For all the success of *Économie et Humanisme*, it was really l'IRFED which gave Lebret a place on the world stage. He became an adviser to several governments and became recognized as an expert on development in what was then called the Third World. His work also came to the attention of the Vatican. In addition to his travels and studies, he was appointed to several United Nations commissions as a representative of the Holy See. In 1963, shortly before the former's death, John XXIII appointed Lebret chief of the Vatican delegation to a UN conference on science, technology, and development. In 1964, Paul VI made him a member of the delegation of the Holy See to a UN conference on commerce and development.[19]

Alongside these responsibilities, Lebret kept a heavy schedule of travel and consultation. From 1962 to 1965, he was involved in constructing development plans in Lebanon, Senegal, Vietnam, Rwanda, and Venezuela, as well as giving lectures all over the world. In 1963, Lebret was invited to be an informal expert at the Second Vatican Council, and in 1964 he became one of the official experts, or *periti,* at the Council. As one of the experts he contributed to the writing of the document that would become *Gaudium et Spes*. In the course of his involvement in Vatican II, Lebret had the opportunity to develop a relationship with Paul VI, who was familiar with many of Lebret's writings.[20]

---

[18] Malley, *Pere Lebret*, 94.
[19] Malley, *Pere Lebret*, 98.
[20] Campanini, "Radici Culturali," 50.

Lebret was a prolific author. He published or collaborated on more than 60 books, articles, and studies in his lifetime, as well as writing for and publishing *Économie et Humanisme*. Paul VI subscribed to this periodical from its inception. His works generally follow two lines. The first are the more spiritually centered works, which focus on theology, prayer, and God's relationship to human beings. *Guide du militant* (1948), *Action, marche vers Dieu* (1949), *Appels du Seigneur (*1957), and *Dimensions de la charité* (1958) are some of these spiritual works, along with several long articles which focus on the examination of conscience.[21]

One of the works that had a significant influence on Paul VI was *Dynamique concrète du développement*. It was written in 1961 and is a study of development patterns in several nations, complete with detailed charts, sophisticated economics graphs, maps, and extensive analysis of the problems brought on by development in each nation.[22] In *Dynamique*, Lebret argues strongly that under-developed countries are frequently under-developed because of exploitation by the West.[23] Societies cannot advance unless they are no longer exploited for economic profit by more economically-sound Western countries, but allowed to turn their resources inward, to concentrate on their own advancement. The necessity of the subordination of one group of countries to another group for progress anywhere in the world is a fable.[24] What is needed is cooperation among countries so that all may benefit from economic progress. When such cooperation is achieved, development will be harmonious, benefitting all, not just a few. The economy must be directed to the service of human beings—this is the "concrete dynamic of development." Set in large boldface type in the French text to emphasize his point, he wrote, "Civilization's problem

---

[21] See Louis-Joseph Lebret, *Guide du militant* (Paris: Efficacité, 1948); *Action, marche vers Dieu* (Paris: Efficacité, 1949); *Appels du Seigneur* (Paris: Editions Ouvrières, 1957); and *Dimensions de la charité* (Paris: Editions Ouvrières, 1958).

[22] Louis-Joseph Lebret, *Dynamique concrète du développement* (Paris: Les éditions ouvrières, 1961). Lebret's *Le drame du siècle*, written near the end of his life, is probably the best synopsis of his thinking and heavily influenced Paul VI. *Le drame du siècle* was both a critique of the path of development the world was taking and a call to genuine cooperation among people and among nations to avert the problems brought on by uneven and often unfair development. While *Le drame du siècle* is one of the few of Lebret's works translated into English, translation problems and heavy redaction make it a distortion and a poor representation of his thought. It is available as *The Last Revolution, the Destiny of Over- and Under-Developed Nations,* trans. John Horgan (New York: Sheed and Ward, 1965).

[23] See Lebret, *Dynamique*, 20: "Fréquemment, dans les pays sous-développés, on considère que l'état de sous-développement est la résultat d'une exploitation directe ou déguisée par l'Occident."

[24] Lebret, *Dynamique*, 21.

is above all a problem of stabilizing man within a generalized regimen of human economy and of harmonized integral development."[25]

Lebret had sounded these themes before, but *Dynamique* is a more complete and comprehensive study than Lebret had previously attempted. He details the differences between the under-developed nations and those that are overdeveloped, having more than they need to sustain themselves. These comparisons include the differences in population, birth and death rates, potable water, incidences of widespread disease, and number of hospitals. In almost all cases, he contends, the underdeveloped countries have needs that are unmet and that could be met with the help of some of the overdeveloped countries.[26]

Near the end of *Dynamique*, Lebret makes two important observations (which are somewhat obscured by his own focus on statistics and charts): people in need are people who will be aggressive to secure those needs,[27] and colonialism, while officially falling apart, is far from dead, as economic exploitation is the new colonialism.[28] Both of these themes were more fully explored in another of Lebret's works, *Le drame du siècle*.

Le drame du siècle is Lebret's call to action for the nations of the world, and is the singular economic work with the most profound influence on *Populorum Progressio*. Portions of at least 11 paragraphs of the encyclical are taken nearly verbatim from this book. Lebret develops several themes, but at the heart of them is a call for a new civilization, a new cooperation between the nations of the world that will ensure coordinated development which meets the crying needs of those who are currently poorer, sicker, and hungrier than those in developed countries. Here, Lebret gives a harsh critique of capitalism and of nations whose economies rely on unchecked capitalism. Capitalism itself is not a problem for Lebret and can be a good economic system, but a laissez-faire capitalism which allows growth and expansion at any cost to the poor for the purpose of making the rich wealthier is an unfair and inhumane system. Capitalism must be channeled, and development must be planned, in order to have an economy which works for all people. It is in this work that Lebret also points out that people and markets are linked across national lines, recognizing what we today would call the global marketplace.

Le drame begins with a summary in narrative form of the information that Lebret laid out in detail in *Dynamique*. The world is unequally developed, and this leads to great riches on the one hand and

---

[25] Lebret, *Dynamique*, 44: "Le problème de civilisation est avant tout un problème de valorisation des hommes dans un régime généralisé d'économie humaine et de développement intégral harmonisé." These are the only words so emphasized in the French text of *Dynamique*.

[26] Lebret, *Dynamique*, 64.

[27] Lebret, *Dynamique*, 422.

[28] Lebret, *Dynamique*, 430.

great poverty on the other, as those who are richer and more economically able exploit those who are poorer and weaker.[29] Not only are riches unequally distributed but so is population, hunger, disease, and early death.

Lebret sees the exploitation of the economically weak by the strong as the new form of imperialism. Colonial powers have ceased to exist in one sense, but they have become even stronger in another, as their former colonies become exploitable resources. The countries of Western Europe (certainly he means the former colonial empires, including his native France) are to blame, but equally to blame is the United States, which is the principal exploiter of developing nations. "The expression 'free world' masks the reality of a world dependent on North American economic power," he writes.[30]

Both Americans and Europeans have become exploitive of others by subscribing to the "fatal error of capitalism": the tendency to forget that economies are not just products and money but involve people as well.[31] Capitalism as practiced in western countries focuses too much on capital and fails to consider the people involved in producing goods or providing raw materials. The people who prosper under capitalism then think that they have prospered of their own accord and forget the many others who have contributed to their prosperity. Another error of capitalism is the tendency to think in the short term and to take the course of action which produces a financial profit quickly. This discourages investment in developing nations, which require long term investment for profitability.

Some of Lebret's harshest words are reserved for what Western nations would term "foreign economic aid" or "foreign development aid." Lebret believes this aid, since it is so insufficient and does not symbolize a true partnership between overdeveloped and underdeveloped nations, is merely a sop to the consciences of those who profit from the current arrangements. This aid is often given with strings attached so that it is not only meant to soothe western consciences but is paternalistic as well.[32] This type of aid is not a mark of true cooperation.

For all of Lebret's criticisms of capitalism, he does not find that Marxism as practiced in the Soviet Union or socialism as practiced in other countries is a better alternative. That is also a development system which forgets the person and exploits the developing world. That

---

[29] Lebret, *Le Drame du Siècle, Misère, Sous-développement, Inconscience, Espoir* (Paris: Les éditions ouvrières, 1960),103-106.
[30] Lebret, *Le Drame du Siècle*, 96: "L' expression de 'monde libre' masque la rèalité d'un monde tributaire de la puissance économique nord-américaine."
[31] Lebret, *Le Drame du Siècle*, 103.
[32] Lebret, *Le Drame du Siècle*, 115-116.

socialism seems to include all peoples is only an illusion, since all things are meant to serve the state, not the people.[33]

Finding both of these systems inappropriate to the creation of a new civilization dedicated to a coordinated and equal distribution of development, Lebret makes his own proposal for a type of "third way" development, based on Christian principles. He calls for cooperation among the nations. The highly developed West must surrender some of its economic power to developing nations, while at the same time helping those nations to achieve a higher level of development. Two percent or more of the wealthier nations' operating budgets, given as aid to developing countries to use as they saw fit within their own situations, would not be too much and would have little impact on the wealthier nations. Wealthier nations are called to help the less affluent in the name of Christian unity but also in the name of the common economic good. The result will be a better, more peaceful world for all. To do less, however, is testimony to the great sin of our time, the greed of nations.[34]

To Lebret, the greatest evil would be to do nothing. "The greatest evil in the world," he wrote, "is not the poverty of the deprived but the indifference of the affluent."[35] Nothing less than a new outlook toward development and developing nations is required for peace to prevail and people worldwide to flourish.

JACQUES MARITAIN

Much more well-known, both contemporaneously and currently, is the work of French philosopher Jacques Maritain (1882-1973). Before his elevation to the papacy, Paul VI had a long relationship with Maritain, beginning shortly before the former's ordination. While still a student, Montini translated Maritain's work *Three Reformers* into Italian in 1925.[36]

Montini may have met Maritain as early as 1924,[37] but the two men came to know each other personally in the 1930s, when Montini was still involved with FUCI, the Italian Catholic university students' group. Montini helped to organize a graduate student group, the *Laureati*, an offshoot of FUCI, in 1936. This group met annually for "study weeks" and studied Maritain, particularly *True Humanism*, which became Maritain's most influential work in Italy. Maritain was chosen for several reasons, chief among them the reality that he was

---

[33] Lebret, *Le Drame du Siècle*, 176.

[34] Lebret, *Le Drame du Siècle*, 116.

[35] Lebret, *Le Drame du Siècle*, 180: "Le plus grande mal du monde n'est pas la pauvreté des démunis mais l'inconscience des nantis."

[36] Jacques Maritain, *Trois Réformateurs, Luther, Descartes, Rousseau, avec six portraits* (Paris: Plon-Nourrit et cie, 1925).

[37] See Peter Hebblethwaite, *Paul VI: The First Modern Pope* (New York: Paulist Press, 1993), 83.

free to speak when others, such as Luigi Sturzo and Alcide de Gasperi, had been silenced by the Fascists when *Laureati* began meeting. Maritain, Sturzo, and others shared many of the same ideas, but only Maritain was free to give voice to them, even though his previous works and speeches had raised controversy in Italy.[38]

When Maritain became ambassador to the Vatican in 1945, he and Montini spent a good deal of time discussing the rise of atheistic humanism, which Maritain believed was what had allowed the extermination of so many people in concentration camps.[39] After Montini was elected pope and decided to continue the Second Vatican Council, he and Maritain again spent time together, often meeting at Castel Gandolfo. During the Council, Maritain was especially concerned with a declaration on the Jews. This had been something he and Paul VI had discussed in depth following the war and again when Maritain was working on the commission which produced the Universal Declaration of Human Rights in 1948.

Late in 1963, Paul VI began preparations for an encyclical that would become *Populorum Progressio*, and he is known to have discussed the plan for this encyclical with Maritain, calling it "an important work" on the themes of development and the place of the church in the development of peoples.[40] (This would be close to the same time he engaged Lebret for some preparatory papers on economics.) While Montini was a student of Maritain, Maritain was not popular with all Italian society. He had been banned from the University of Milan in 1934 after one of his speeches on religion and culture, and his works caused controversy among Italian intellectuals, who either saw him as a sort of prophet, as Montini did, or as a troublemaker who was best kept quiet.[41] At Vatican II, some, including the still-formidable Alfredo Ottaviani, wanted Maritain's Christian humanism condemned, along with the works of such theologians as Henri de Lubac and Pierre Teilhard de Chardin.[42] It is telling, then, that Paul VI chose to showcase not only de Lubac and other *ressourcement* theologians in *Populorum Progressio* but also quoted from Maritain's *True Humanism* twice. Coupled with the honor Paul VI had given to Maritain at the close of the Second Vatican Council, this was a clear papal signal that Maritain's Christian humanism was not to be condemned but embraced.

---

[38] Hebblethwaite, *Paul VI,* 122. Also see Giorgio Campanini, "Montini e Maritain," in *G. B. Montini e la Società Italiana 1919-1939* (Brescia, Italy: Centro di Documentazione, 1985), 88-90.

[39] Phillipe Chenaux, *Paul VI et Maritain, les rapports du "Montinianisme" et du "Maritainisme,"* (Brescia, Italy: Istituto Paolo VI, 1994), 42.

[40] Chenaux, *Paul VI et Maritain,* 90.

[41] Campanini, "Montini e Maritain," 88-92.

[42] Hebblethwaite, *Paul VI,* 287.

Unlike Lebret, who was directly involved in the composition of *Populorum Progressio* and therefore had his own work incorporated into the text, Maritain was a subtler influence on the composition of the encyclical. Of particular interest to the composition of *Populorum Progressio* is Maritain's *Humanisme intégral, problèmes temporels et spirituels d'une nouvelle chrétienté*, first published in 1936. Paul VI had studied this work in depth and its influence on him can be seen in the deeper themes of his encyclical.

L'humanisme intégral, by far the most significant of Maritain's works for *Populorum Progressio*, was published in French in 1936 and translated into English as *True Humanism* in 1938.[43] It is a collection of six lectures given by Maritain at the University of Santander in 1934, and compiled together with an introduction. These lectures represent Maritain's view of the human person and human society, including the direction each of these is taking and should take. This is probably the one work of Maritain's which had the most influence on Paul VI, and he began studying it soon after its publication in French. Maritain argues in this work that a genuine or a true humanism cannot be divorced from transcendence, from the sense that there is something supra-human that is beyond human abilities. This humanism is inseparable from civilization and culture, which are expressions of humanism. Any true philosophy of humanism must be "integral," incorporating all the facets of the human being—social, economic, cultural, religious—and grounded in respect for human dignity and "the rights of human personality."[44]

Maritain sees a historical shift since the end of the Middle Ages and the beginning of the Reformation away from a humanism that is theocentric, one which places God at the center of human endeavor, and toward a humanism that is anthropocentric, one that believes that human beings are at the center of all things. "This first kind of humanism," he writes,

> recognizes that the centre for man is God; it implies the Christian conception of man as at once a sinner and redeemed, and the Christian conception of grace and freedom, whose principles we have already called to mind. The second kind of humanism believes that man is his own centre, and therefore the centre of all things. It implies a naturalistic conception of man and of freedom.[45]

---

[43] Jacques Maritain, *L'humanisme integral* (Paris: Aubier, 1936) and *True Humanism* (London: Geoffrey Bles, New York: Charles Scribner's Sons, 1938). There are many English editions of this work. The translation referred to in this essay is the edition referenced in footnote 44 of *Populorum Progressio*.

[44] Maritain, *True Humanism*, xvii.

[45] Maritain, *True Humanism*, 19.

This anthropocentric humanism focuses on the temporal, the world which will eventually end in destruction, to the detriment of the spiritual, the incarnational aspect of humanity that will endure. Such a humanism is mistaken, and, more than mistaken, it is inhuman. This is the result of philosophy which has turned to the scientific and away from the spiritual. The extreme results of an anthropocentric humanism can be seen in atheism, especially Soviet atheism, for which Maritain has many condemnations. This "socialist humanism" subverts individuality, taking away the personhood of the human being in service to the good of the collective set of human beings. Of the Soviet version of humanism, Maritain writes,

> It is a question for it of changing man so as to oust the transcendent God of whom he is an image, of creating a human being who will be in himself the god, lacking no supra-temporal attribute, of history and his titanic dynamism, a human being who must first of all be de-individualized, whose joy will be in his devotion to all, in being an organ of the revolutionary community, in expectation of the day when he will find on the triumph of the collective man over nature a transfigured personality.[46]

A person is not really a person in this philosophy but rather a part of the state, which orders all things to its own survival. Communism is denounced, but Maritain also offers a strong critique of capitalism as a materialist universe, one in which the human being is not a person but a consumer, a part of the engine that drives the capitalist society. This can be as debasing to the human person as communism, even though many capitalist societies allow freedom for spirituality.

Both communistic and capitalistic philosophies call out for radical changes in the temporal order, a transformation which will allow people to once again understand their spirituality and return to a more theocentric humanism which allows for the growth of the human person but is still focused on God and the Kingdom of God. Maritain writes:

> The social and political philosophy implied by integral humanism calls for radical changes in our actual system of culture ... a substantial transformation. And this transformation demands, not only the inauguration of new social structures and a new scheme of social life succeeding that of capitalism, but also (and consubstantially) a rousing of forces of faith, of intelligence and of love in the inner depths of the soul, an advance in the discovery of spiritual realities. Only on these conditions can man truly enter more

---

[46] Maritain, *True Humanism*, 54.

profoundly into the deep planes of his nature without mu-
tilating or disfiguring it.[47]

These radical changes amount to a "new Christendom," a new
Christian ordering of society, politics, and economics. As Maritain
himself puts it, the new Christendom will be "a temporal system or
age of civilization whose animating form will be Christian and which
will correspond to the historical climate of the epoch on whose thresh-
old we are."[48] The new Christendom would not be confined to one
country but, like Christendom of old, would encircle the world.

This new Christendom encompassed several points. First, it was to
be pluralistic, incorporating economic and religious diversity in recognition of the autonomy and freedom of the human person. Although
the human person is rightly oriented to God as the center of all things,
faith cannot be forced but must be approached in freedom. This plu-
ralism and freedom contributes to the common good by allowing all
the opportunity to know their theocentric humanity in their own way.
Most importantly, it is not to be an authoritarian state in any way.[49]

Although grounded in Christian principles, the new Christendom
would be secular, led by lay people, not the institutional church. This
is not an anti-religious state but one which is grounded in the dignity
of the human person and constructs a temporal order which is indica-
tive of that dignity. The common good in the temporal order would be
an end in itself, though only an intermediate end and subordinate to
the spiritual ends of humankind. A Christian secular state which recognizes the essential humanity of all members of society can construct
a just social system in which all may participate, not just those who
hold authority. This is in sharp contrast to the current regimes of communism, which concentrates authority in a few who may then subju-
gate the many, and capitalism, which does not recognize each person's
humanity within the profit/loss system. After the end of capitalism and
the establishment of this Christian secular state, the common good
would involve the common ownership of some parts of society, including the common ownership—and profit from—the means of production.[50]

Maritain envisions the new Christendom as a "concrete historical
ideal," a vision to be worked for through concrete actions in the temporal sphere.[51] Human beings need to choose between a system which
dehumanizes them and makes them subject to science and rationalism
and a system which recognizes their essential humanity and allows for

---

[47] Maritain, *True Humanism*, 82.
[48] Maritain, *True Humanism*, 126.
[49] Maritain, *True Humanism*, 156-204.
[50] Maritain, *True Humanism*, 205-222.
[51] Maritain, *True Humanism*, 121.

the re-emergence of the theocentric humanism which is the proper way of seeing the world. Such a transformation will require work, hard work, in political, social, and economic spheres. But this "concrete historical ideal" of the new Christendom is worth the work, because it is the ideal to which all people are called, for the realization of the fulfillment of humanity. He writes,

> Indeed there is nothing which rouses more scandal and, in a sense, is more revolutionary…than the belief in a form of political action which is intrinsically Christian in its principles, in its spirit, in its methods, and the claim to advance the world to a form of political action which is vitally Christian. But the man conscious of these things knows that the first way of serving the common good is to remain faithful to the values of truth, of justice, of love which are its principal element.[52]

FUTURE DIRECTIONS FOR THE STUDY OF *POPULORUM PROGRESSIO*

The marriage of Lebret's thinking on economics and development and their connection to human flourishing and Maritain's integral humanism is one of the truly original and significant contributions of *Populorum Progressio*. While much had been written, both within and outside the Church, on economics and the responsibilities of various actors, it is *Populorum Progressio* which ties economic development and the complete development of the human person together as intrinsically related and inseparable. The concepts introduced by *Populorum Progressio* were relevant in their own context in 1967 and have become even more relevant in the 50 years since, as economic globalization has forced the issues of exploitation, economic colonization, and inequality ever more to the surface. As issues like these become more important in a globalized economy, *Populorum Progressio* can continue to offer a moral direction for the future of development, both economic and human. To hear this voice, however, requires an ongoing engagement with the document so that its insights can be better connected to the wider tradition of economic and social teachings. Just as *Rerum Novarum* and other encyclicals from the tradition are applied to new or ongoing situations, so must *Populorum Progressio* be one of the first places to turn for guidance on globalization, poverty, and inequality.

The way forward for scholarship on *Populorum Progressio* is defined as much by what is missing as by what has already been written on the document. A lack of resources restricts scholarship on every level. Of particular concern is the lack of resources available on the work of Lebret. A fuller understanding of Paul VI's document de-

---

[52] Maritain, *True Humanism*, 260.

mands a deeper understanding of Lebret's life and work, his publications, and his connections to worker movements and other Catholic movements in France and throughout the world. While Maritain's work and connection to *Populorum Progressio* is well known, Lebret has not become nearly as widely analyzed. Though not unknown outside of his native France, much of his work remains unavailable to scholars in North America. Most university libraries do not shelve copies of his most influential works, likely because they are out of print and have never been translated to English. Until recently, he did not even merit an English-language Wikipedia page. Although there is some scholarship on Lebret and his work, much of it is older than *Populorum Progressio* itself and only available on a limited basis through European libraries. Cost and availability certainly have been contributing factors restricting needed scholarship in this regard.

The lack of resources also offers a somewhat unique opportunity for scholars to pursue projects on *Populorum Progressio* in conjunction with colleagues around the world. The document itself stresses the need for "mutual collaboration and a heightened sense of solidarity," which is likely to be fruitful not just in relationships between nations but also in relationships between scholars. The problems of accessing materials and translating them to a useable format can be overcome with the aid of colleagues in other nations where such materials exist. More importantly, collaborative work opens possibilities for mutual understanding that is in the spirit of the document itself. Reaching across the bounds of language, nation, and institution can lead not only to better understanding on all sides but to a true solidarity among scholars. Just as there are wealthy nations and those that have less, there are well-off institutions and those that have far fewer resources. If it is imperative for wealthy nations and under-developed ones to work together for the better development of all, can we not say the same for all scholars? Such collaboration can only lead to the same end imagined by Paul VI, an interdependence based on mutual solidarity that contributes greatly to the good of all. Ⓜ

Journal of Moral Theology, Vol. 6, No. 1 (2017): 21-38

The Soul of Development

Clemens Sedmak

HE KEY IS TO FIND LOCAL LEADERS who own the dream and will make it happen," American banker Jacqueline Novogratz remarked against the background of her experience with development work in Africa.[1] Dreams and desires, they are part of the inner state of a person, and authentic development according to Catholic social teaching depends upon the inner state of the human person. In this paper, I explore this connection between the inner state and development in the light of Catholic Social Tradition, primarily focusing on *Populorum Progressio*. I first examine the immaterial dimension of development, then how these elements can be considered a "soul" for Catholic social teaching, and finally the development priorities that emerge in the light of this understanding.

THE IMMATERIAL DIMENSION OF DEVELOPMENT

Stacey Edgar founded an organization importing hand-made African crafts to the United States. Her organization

> openly shares the stories of every group making our products and believes that the only way buying habits change is when people see the things they buy as not just "things" but as the people behind those items. This gives women the chance to connect, to learn about women's lives abroad and see their hard work and talents flowing out through the beautiful products they made, and to know that each purchase directly affects the life of the woman who made that product.[2]

Edgar's work indicates that a thing is more than a thing. "Things," or objects, are not flat. They have an outside and an inside representing certain values. Things have something to say and have both message and meaning beyond their tangible surface.

This is something that the British anthropologist Daniel Miller has studied.[3] Miller looked at the subjective value of household articles in

---

[1] Jacqueline Novogratz, *The Blue Sweater* (New York: Rodale, 2009), 34.
[2] Stacey Edgar, *Global Girlfriends* (New York: St. Martin's Press, 2011), 51.
[3] See Daniel Miller, *The Comfort of Things* (Cambridge: Polity, 2009) and *Stuff* (Cambridge: Polity, 2010).

homes in one street in East London. The things people have in their homes are not as "inanimate" as they might look but impact the behavior and attitudes of the people around them (their "owners"). They provide and "profound" the stories they are part of and give meaning – add soul – to the human lives they share.[4]

Development also entails an interior aspect. According to Catholic Social Teaching, authentic development is linked to personal growth (*Sollicitudo Rei Socialis*, no. 6) and seeks the development of the whole person (no. 14). All dimensions of the human person need to be addressed (no. 1), including the inner dimension. In order for development to be authentic, it has to be understood as a spiritual, moral, cultural and social term rather than just an economic one: economic growth is dependent on social progress (no. 35), and there is a central ethical and cultural dimension of development (no. 8) with an undeniable moral element (no. 33). "Development which is merely economic is incapable of setting man free; on the contrary, it will end by enslaving him further" (no. 46). In other words, there is always a non-observable dimension to the observable, a non-material dimension to the material.

The foundation of the Church's understanding of development is the dignity of the human person. The Catholic understanding of human dignity emphasizes both a material and a non-material dimension. In *Populorum Progressio*, Pope Paul VI discusses the material goals of development: to ensure a decent life; to escape hunger, poverty, endemic disease and ignorance; to share in the benefits of civilization; to improve human qualities; and to strive for fuller growth (no. 1). However, Catholic Social Teaching and *Populorum Progressio*'s perspective on dignity go beyond the material to the non-material dimension to include a sense of interiority and inwardness. The goal of a humane and humanely decent life is reached once discrimination has been eliminated, the human person liberated from the bonds of servitude, and people given "the capacity, in the sphere of temporal realities, to improve their lot, to further their moral growth and to develop their spiritual endowments" (*Populorum Progressio*, no. 34).

Human dignity is linked to self-fulfillment. This link can be reconstructed in the exhortation of *Populorum Progressio* with the idea that a person is responsible for self-fulfillment (no. 150). It is another way of saying that the human person has a duty to do something with the life they have been given, that "human self-fulfillment may be said to sum up our obligations" (no. 16).[5] There are guidelines as to the real-

---

[4] See Russell Belk, "Possessions and the Extended Self," *The Journal of Consumer Research* 15, no. 2 (1988): 139-168.

[5] Ronald Dworkin has expressed this duty to self-realization from a different angle in his *Justice for Hedgehogs* (Massachusetts: Harvard University Press, 2011).

ization of this duty (nos. 16, 18) and there is a clear telos of the realization of this duty: the highest goal of human self-fulfillment is "a new fullness of life" (no. 16). The notion of "fullness of life" is not a term used to express developmental minimalism or a sufficientism. It is not enough to cover "basic needs." It is not enough to ensure human survival. The goal of development that takes the dignity of each human person seriously is not modest but ambitious. Proper development has to happen "from within"; "soulless development" misses the very point of the human person. Thus, the ultimate goal of development is a full-bodied humanism (no. 41), a humanism that points the way to God (no. 42).[6]

Catholic Social Teaching emphasizes the primacy of the immaterial over the material. Material goods and material development have to serve immaterial (moral and spiritual) development. Furthermore, there can be no proper material growth without proper spiritual growth, no proper development without moral and spiritual development. We will need a new way of thinking if we are to bring about a change and renewal of proper development (*Caritas in Veritate*, no. 53), since development depends on inner attitudes (*Sollicitudo Rei Socialis*, no. 38). As Pope Benedict XVI wrote in *Caritas in Veritate*, "Paul VI, in his encyclical letter *Populorum Progressio*, pointed out that the causes of underdevelopment are not primarily of the material order. He invited us to search for them in other dimensions of the human person: first of all, in the will, which often neglects the duties of solidarity; secondly in thinking, which does not always give proper direction to the will" (no. 19). *Populorum Progressio* articulates and applies a principle of prudence in its repeated invitations to a culture of thoughtfulness, in its invitation of deep thought and the reflection of the wise (no. 20). The encyclical sees thoughtfulness as the proper response to developmental challenges and makes an appeal in its favor (no. 85). The encyclical also prioritizes wisdom over knowledge. Experts with their specialized knowledge are important agents in development work, but they "must realize that their expert knowledge does not give them superiority in every sphere of life" (no. 72). Proper development needs more than planning. It needs wisdom.

POPULORUM PROGRESSIO AND
THE INNER DIMENSION OF THE PERSON

Development in Catholic Social Teaching has to start with the understanding of the priority of the immaterial over the material, "with

---

[6] The version of humanism is shaped by the thinking of Jacques Maritain. See Joseph M. De Torre, "Maritain's 'Integral Humanism' and Catholic Social Teaching," in *Reassessing the Liberal State: Reading Maritain's Man and the State*, eds. T. Fuller and J. P. Hittinger (Washington, DC: Catholic University of America Press, 2001), 202-208.

the interior freedom that men must find again with regard to their goods and their powers" (*Octogesima Adveniens*, no. 45). As *Sollicitudo Rei Socialis* explicitly considers, "Development which is not only economic must be measured and oriented according to the reality and vocation of man seen in his totality, namely, according to his interior dimension" (no. 29). In the following section, I explore the connection between interiority and development more deeply, focusing on the various ways *Populorum Progressio* uses aspects of that interior life of the human person to discuss and define development.

Private Property

While *Populorum Progressio* reiterates the principle of the social nature of private property, it goes one notch higher in transferring it to the level of nation-states. Paul VI writes, "We must repeat that the superfluous goods of wealthier nations ought to be placed at the disposal of poorer nations" (no. 49). This notion is remarkable since it connects the micro-level of individual agents with a macro-level of nations or states without any further hermeneutical justification or effort. The underlying philosophical idea could be termed "permeability," in the sense that terms and ideas on a lower level also hold on a higher level.[7]

We see this principle of permeability at work when we read about micro-categories such as dialogue being applied to inter-state relations (*Populorum Progressio*, no. 54) or explicitly when the just wage motif from *Rerum Novarum*, no. 43 is transferred to trade relations (*Populorum Progressio*, no. 59). We also see the effortless transfer from micro-level language to macro-level dimensions at play when the document talks about nations being "jealous" (nos. 49, 52, 62). The language used in the encyclical to describe relationships among nations is the language one would use to talk about interpersonal relationships and friendships.

Love

Development in Catholic social teaching is linked to an expression of love. For *Populorum Progressio*, love leads to the willingness to make sacrifices (no. 47) which are necessary if re-distribution is to become real. The readiness to pay higher taxes, for example, can be seen as an expression of love (no. 47). Educators should inspire young people "with a love for the needy nations" (no. 83). Clearly, the concept of "love" emerges as the key notion: "It is the person who is motivated by genuine love, more than anyone else, who pits his intelligence against the problems of poverty" (no. 75) and "only in charity,

---

[7] Clemens Sedmak, "Utility and Identity: A Catholic Social Teaching Perspective on the *Economics of Good and Evil*," *Studies in Christian Ethics* 28, no. 4 (2015): 461-477.

illumined by the light of reason and faith, is it possible to pursue development goals that possess a more humane and humanizing value" (*Caritas in Veritate*, no. 9). Underdevelopment happens because of an erosion of "brotherly ties between individuals and nations" (*Populorum Progressio*, no. 66). Knowledge without love will obstruct rather than enhance development: the role of experts is important, but "the expert's message will surely be rejected by these people if it is not inspired by brotherly love" (no. 71).

In addition, *Populorum Progressio* explicitly refers to the human heart. It notes that people under certain circumstances and life-experiences will "harden their hearts" (no. 19),[8] while the ferment of the Gospel can "arouse in man's heart the irresistible requirements of his dignity" (no. 32). A union "of mind and heart" is the road to proper development (nos. 27, 80), and it is this goal of the unification of minds and hearts to which economic progress should aspire (no. 35).

Memory, Desires, and the Intellect

Populorum Progressio also discusses development in terms of the human faculties of memory, desires, and the intellect. Memory is mentioned in the discussion of the appropriation of the past (nos. 7, 10, 40, 62, 68). There is a clear emphasis on the importance of a proper ethics of memory, a proper way of remembering. Proper development calls for an ethics of memory: a proper way of not forgetting, a proper way of cultivating common remembering, and an effort to preserve cultural memory in a communicative way.

Populorum Progressio discusses the importance of personal desires in attaining growth (no. 15) and shaping development (nos. 21, 32-33, 64). It is similar to how Edgar talks about the role of proper desires in connection to African products. She teaches African artisans to make and sell products that are desirable by American standards and not bought out of pity. Otherwise, the artisans cannot survive market challenges, will go on depending on non-profit organizations, and continue to produce "giraffes, which sat in church basements across the nation until next year's sale."[9] *Populorum Progressio* even looks into emotional nationalism (no. 62) and into racism with its seemingly inevitable companion emotions of bitterness (no. 63).

Populorum Progressio emphasizes intelligence and the power of thought (no. 27), the weight of giving thought and consideration to questions of development (no. 85). Ideas are needed to ensure and enhance integral development (no. 5). Ideas (or epistemic commitments)

---

[8] In a similar vein, see Novogratz, *Blue Sweater*, 41 where she mentions the difficulties of working in Rwanda, "thinking about the paradoxes of a physically spectacular country having a soul punctured by the competing forces of racism, colonialism, development and geographic isolation."

[9] Edgar, *Global Girlfriends*, 42.

are the basis for human behaviour: "every form of social action involves some doctrine" (no. 39). There is an intangible infrastructure of values, ideas, and knowledge underlying the tangible infrastructure of a country. This is explicitly expressed in no. 40, which talks about the cultural tradition of every country: "This tradition includes institutions required by life in the world, and higher manifestations—artistic, intellectual and religious—of the life of the spirit." The section praises the importance of these immaterial aspects of a country's infrastructure and quotes Mt 16:26 ("What profit would there be for one to gain the whole world and forfeit his life?"). Consequently, *Populorum Progressio* discusses the importance of "awareness" (nos. 9, 21). Thus, it warns against the dangers of totalitarian ideologies (no. 11) and of missionary thought patterns that may get in the way of proclaiming the good news (no. 12).

Moral Language

The central role of the inner is also made visible in the encyclical's application of interpersonal moral language to the national and international level. The language of temptation is used in correlation to nations in *Populorum Progressio*, no. 41. People are "tempted by the alluring but deceitful promises of would-be saviors" (no. 11). Some people are "sorely tempted" to make use of violent means (no. 30). We find the language of the virtues, especially generosity (no. 54), which leads to "willing sacrifice" (no. 47). *Populorum Progressio* addresses the dangers of the vice of avarice (no. 18) stating, "Avarice, in individuals and in nations, is the most obvious form of stultified moral development" (no. 19). This echoes early Christian warnings that avarice is a fundamental and principal fault of the soul, an evil that breeds further evil (1 Tim 6:10). In connection with nations, the encyclical also discusses various forms of pride: "stubborn pride" (no. 53), "haughty pride" (nos. 62, 82), and "nationalistic pride" (no. 72). Paul VI even discusses the destructive jealousy of and between nations (nos. 49, 52, 62, 76).

Moral Poverty

Populorum Progressio describes "moral poverty" as the poverty of those "crushed under the weight of their own self-love" (no. 20). This immoderate self-love poses a major obstacle to proper development (no. 82), as it is a consideration of self at the expense of others, embracing a model of bettering one's own position by weakening the position of others. Self-love is immoderate if it does not recognize limits, such as the social limits of private property or the communal limits of personal desires. Immoderate self-love frequently translates into structural sin, as sin committed by thoughtless or inconsiderate human agents and consolidated in structures.[10] In this way, selfishness can become petrified and translated into structural realities.

Moral poverty is overcome with the gift of faith (no. 21) and the invitation to trust in God (no. 37). This commitment to the immaterial can be fostered by material prosperity since the mind is then (ideally) less burdened with material worries (no. 41) and by fighting unfair conditions as these actions further a person's spiritual and moral development (no. 76). However, truly human conditions that overcome moral poverty are linked to "refinement and culture" (no. 21) and the development of "taste" (no. 21). The category "taste" indicates that development cannot be reduced to hard factors and is inextricably linked to culture and "cultivation." "Taste" is not unrelated to external developments, as Pierre Bourdieu has famously discussed,[11] but is clearly an expression of subtlety in between a merely bodily response and rational judgments.

THE SOUL OF DEVELOPMENT

Together, these aspects of *Populorum Progressio* make ample use of the inner life of the human being to describe development and so constitute a kind of "soul" for it. The soul stands for and characterizes "the innermost aspect of man, that which is of greatest value in him, that by which he is most especially in God's image: 'soul' signifies the spiritual principle in man" (*Catechism of the Catholic Church*, no. 363). The soul constitutes the indestructible core of a human person, the inner center of her identity.

Christian authors have put forward what could be called a "thick conception of interiority." They developed a rich language to talk about the inner life, a language which may include terms such as "movements," "purity," "beauty," "demons," "temptations," "battles," and "struggles." Contributions to the rich language of the soul can be found in early Christian writings, but St. Augustine's *Confessions* provides a decisive influence on the development of the notion of inwardness[12] and a key work in the historical development of the understanding of the soul. The imagery Augustine uses to illustrate inwardness of being is revealing: the house (Bk 1.5), the heart as vessel (Bk 10.35), arable land (Bk 2.3), the image of the battleground (Bk 8.8). This inner space of interiority is, according to Augustine, the "core" of the human being. It is that inner space in which we can find God and the place "where God makes himself known to me" (Bk 1.2). Inner

---

[10] See Pope John Paul II, *Paenitentia et Reconciliatio*, no. 16 for the relationship between personal sin and social sin; see John M. Breen, "John Paul II, The Structures of Sin and The Limits of Law," *Saint Louis University Law Journal* 52, no. 317 (2008): 318-73, especially 333-338.

[11] Pierre Bourdieu, *Distinction* (London: Routledge, 1984), especially chapter 5.

[12] See Peter Carey, *Augustine's Invention of the Inner Self* (New York: Oxford University Press, 2000).

being resonates with the dynamics of our aspirations and desires, memories past and conclusions drawn, the sense of joy and the sense of despair. Thus, the soul as inner space can be depicted as "active agent" as well as backdrop where the events of life are "staged" and come to pass.

As immeasurable as our inner being may be, it is not without structure. It is the seat of diverse powers (will, memory, reason) but also divergent moods and emotions: craving and lust, joy, fear, regret and grief (Bk 10.14). In his tenth book, Augustine reserves a special place for memory – *memoria* – as part of inner being and the basis for developing a concept of self. He claims that it is memory that drives the thinking process (Bk 10.11). He is continually amazed by that rich inner homogeneity of memory which harnesses the heterogeneity of thought. Memory plays a central role in Augustine's analysis of the heart of being and the core of interiority; it is the place in which we are confronted by ourselves (Bk 10.8). The soul, then, emerges in this rich language as "place" and "agent" and "core" and as the "home" of intellect, will, memory, attitudes and emotions.

We have seen that *Populorum Progressio* underscores many elements of Augustine's understanding of the soul. A proper attitude to development that does not dismiss the idea of human interiority in general or the idea of the soul in particular will pay serious attention to those inner forces of emotions and desires, thoughts and judgments, memories and attitudes. The pivotal claim in Augustine is that the soul *is* structured and *can* be structured; it follows an order. This point is not only important for questions of spiritual growth but also for development in all its dimensions.

In some ways, the inner dimension of the human person as meaningful and essential is already found in certain thoughts on development. The role of emotions in politics is an area finally being addressed and discussed seriously.[13] There is also the idea of religion to be considered, an idea which Leah Selinger calls "the forgotten factor" in development,[14] a factor which regards religions as players in development work. If development efforts set out to make use of all available resources and if development seriously intends to consider *all* dimensions of the human person, then, undoubtedly, there is a need to consider religion.[15] Efforts have been made to "rewrite the secular

---

[13] Martha Nussbaum, *Political Emotions* (Massachusetts: Harvard UP, 2013); Todd Hall, *Emotional Diplomacy* (New York: Cornell University Press, 2015).

[14] Leah Selinger, "The Forgotten Factor: The Uneasy Relationship Between Religion and Development," *Social Compass* 51, no. 4 (2004): 523-543.

[15] Erik Meyersson, *Religion, Politics and Development* (Stockholm: Stockholm University Press, 2010); Gerrie Ter Haar, ed., *Religion and Development: Ways of Transforming the world* (London: Hurst and Co., 2011); Scott M. Thomas, *The Global Resurgence of Religion and the Transformation of International Relations: The Struggle for the Soul of the Twenty-First Century* (Basingstoke, UK: Palgrave

script" of development, especially by Severine Deneulin.[16] Even the World Bank has adopted approaches to accommodate the role of religion.[17]

But any consideration of the inner must not stop at "the obvious consideration" of religions in their institutional dimension. Development work that takes interiority into account in the spirit of *Populorum Progressio* will have to pay special attention to its Augustine-like soul. Three people exemplify this approach. First, Martin Kaempchen is a German Christian who has been working in a village outside of Calcutta for more than four decades, doing development work in the villages of Ghosaldanga and Bishnubati.[18] He acknowledges how deep conversations can open up a sense of possibilities, a horizon of possible scenarios for the future, the idea that things could be different from what they have been and what they are. Kaempchen laments the lack of mental flexibility, of creativity, and imagination on the side of the poor.[19] Education is a process that offers points of reference and contextualization enabling people to make judgments. Without an educational background, village life becomes the benchmark norm. Literacy opens up a world beyond hitherto perceived experience and senses, beyond the moment. Literacy is a world of abstract representations in a mundane world of concrete reality. Because of this lack of judgment, "school" is not an investment in the future but an institution depriving a household of important laborers.

This basic attitude towards education is one of the major obstacles standing in the way of development, in Kaempchen's view. Poverty is like "a mental cage" that prevents people from identifying (let alone realizing) their potential. Judgments are based on emotions and first sight impressions. In other words, village life reflects judgments which again reflect the inner state of the villagers. "Fatalism" in this context is not so much patience and endurance as lack of a sense of initiative, a lack of the judgment that the world can be changed by proper agency.[20] Kaempchen sees the poor as their own worst enemies

---

MacMillan, 2005); Philip Van Ufford and Matthew Shoffeleers, eds., *Religion and Development: Towards an Integrated Approach* (Amsterdam: Free University Press, 1988).

[16] Severine Deneulin and Carole Rakodi, "Revisiting Religion: Development Studies Thirty Years On," *World Development* 39, no. 1 (2001): 45-54; Severine Deneulin with Masooda Bano, *Religion in Development: Rewriting the Secular Script* (London and New York: Zed Books, 2009); see also Jenny Lunn, "The Role of Religion, Spirituality and Faith in Development: A Critical Theory Approach," *Third World Quarterly* 30, no. 5 (2009): 937-951.

[17] Katherine Marshall and Marisa Van Saanen, *Development and Faith: Where Mind, Heart and Soul Work Together* (Washington, DC: The World Bank, 2007).

[18] Martin Kämpchen, *Leben ohne Armut. Wie Hilfe wirklich helfen kann – meine Erfahrungen in Indien* (Freiburg/Breisgau: Herder, 2011).

[19] Kämpchen, *Leben ohne Armut*, 36.

[20] Kämpchen, *Leben ohne Armut*, 44.

in many instances due to their incapacity to make proper, well-deliberated judgments. Hence, he sees poverty primarily as a mental state.[21] Clearly, development is linked to questions of the intellectual dimension of the person, hardly anyone would doubt that, so it would seem that this fact strengthens the link between development work and the inner "stage" of the person, between development and "the soul."

Greg Mortsensen's work provides a second example of taking the soul as central to development. In his classical account *Three Cups of Tea*, he tells the story of the beginnings of his efforts to build a school in a Pakistani village.[22] He has two reasons for wanting to build the school: indebtedness and shock. Both strengthen his commitment. Mortensen was indebted to the inhabitants of Korphe for nursing him back to life after a failed attempt to climb K2. After his recuperation, he was shocked to find out that the village did not have a school. Hence, the major force driving his commitment to change was personal involvement. He "couldn't imagine ever discharging the debt he felt to his hosts in Korphe. But he was determined to try."[23] He was deeply impressed by the children's desire to learn, and this, in turn, generated his own desire to help. This desire was reinforced by the memory of his sister Christa who had died a few months before his K2 expedition. The children of Korphe reminded Mortensen of Christa. They reminded him that his sister had had to fight for so many things others took for granted. Against this background Mortensen made a solemn promise, "I will build a school."[24]

Mortensen's commitment was strong. He wrote 580 letters asking for help, and the outcome was one negative reply. He tried to save money by living frugally. The turning point in his own efforts to help came from the Swiss entrepreneur and scientist Jean Hoerni, who had heard about Mortensen's attempt to build a school in a Pakistani village and wanted to support it. Hoerni – another story of commitment – was especially fond of Pakistan where he had wonderful memories of trekking in the past. He sent a twelve thousand-dollar check to Mortensen, "and a brief note scrawled on a piece of folded graph paper: 'Don't screw up. Regards, J.H.'"[25] This was the breakthrough as $12,000 was the amount that Mortensen had calculated necessary for the school project. And then the story – with its many complications – unfolded. The crucial factor was Mortensen's commitment, his desire to help, his will.

---

[21] Kämpchen, *Leben ohne Armut*, 50.

[22] Greg Mortensen (with David Oliver Relin), *Three Cups of Tea* (London: Penguin, 2007).

[23] Mortensen, *Three Cups of Tea*, 30.

[24] Mortensen, *Three Cups of Tea*, 33.

[25] Mortensen, *Three Cups of Tea*, 55.

Finally, Liane Philips works to support the long term unemployed or never employed people with no access to the labor market in Ohio.[26] She identifies inner obstacles in the clients with whom she works. She pinpoints tough barriers such as fear, poor self-esteem, lack of self-confidence, feelings of powerlessness, and inappropriate attitudes standing in the way of development.[27] Poverty forces a person to constantly operate in crisis or survival mode. This mode has to do with memory dynamics: "When you've been in poverty a long time, your memory bank is full of deposits, but they aren't the kind of deposits that you can draw on to move ahead."[28] Experiences fill a person's memory banks. If experiences have been difficult or even traumatic, those memory banks will be shaped in a particular way and because of the plasticity of the memory new experiences will be interpreted against this background. "Healing memories," an "ethics of memory", thus becomes an important element in development work.

THE SOUL AND DEVELOPMENT PRIORITIES

One of the ongoing challenges of moral discourse in general and development in particular is that of priorities. Problems can rarely if ever all be tackled simultaneously, let alone in tandem. There are the opportunity costs of development work and poverty alleviation to consider (e.g., the decision between "today versus tomorrow," "deep versus broad," and "symptoms versus causes"). Any strategies of prioritization will ultimately depend on the underlying concept of development. The question of priority-setting is particularly relevant for the Least Developed Countries (LDC). The concept of the soul—especially Augustine's idea that the soul *is* structured and *can* be structured—helps to organize development priorities.

The Istanbul Programme agreed upon at the Fourth United Nations Conference on Least Developed Countries in 2014 reflects the full spectrum of the challenge of development.[29] The overarching goal of the Istanbul Programme of Action is to overcome the structural challenges faced by the least developed countries, to eradicate poverty, achieve internationally agreed upon development goals, and enable half of the 48 least developed countries to graduate out of this category by 2020. The Istanbul Program identifies five primary objectives for

---

[26] Lianne Phillips and Echo Montgomery Garrett, *Why Don't They Just Get a Job?* (Texas: aha! Process Inc., 2010).

[27] Phillips and Garrett, *Why Don't They Just Get a Job?*, 54-55.

[28] Phillips and Garrett, *Why Don't They Just Get a Job?*, 131.

[29] Fourth United Nations Conference on the Least Developed Countries, "Programme of Action for the Least Developed Countries for the Decade 2011-2020," ldc4istanbul.org/uploads/IPoA.pdf; See also the 2014 background paper for this by Mehmet Arda, *Least Developed Countries – Development Priorities and Development Cooperation*, www.idc-istanbul2014.org/notes/istanbul-19-20-june-2014-background-paper-ldcs-development-priorities-and-development-cooperation.pdf.

this time period: economic growth, human capacity-building, reduction of vulnerability, financial resources management, and good governance. The United Nations Office of the High Representative for the Least Developed presented an additional report on priority-setting suggesting debt reduction, poverty reduction, access to new technologies, economic growth and the development of agriculture as key priorities.[30] The LDC Independent Expert Group on the Post-2015 Development Agenda has also issued a report on priorities for LDC, which aims to inform and support negotiations for the next development framework.[31] The Expert Group has identified a framework for the post-2015 development agenda around the concept of solidarity and which highlights five strengths of the LDC that can be mobilized for sustainable development: resilient societies; good local governance; innovation; environmental stewardship; cultural and traditional values. The Independent Expert Group also identified six key priorities: (1) respect for their (LDC's) sovereignty and the decisions they want to make, (2) equity and democracy in international structures (trade regimes, institutions), (3) a new definition of development cooperation based on respect and what the LDC really need, (4) increasing global income equity, (5) a more equal distribution of natural resources, in particular the natural resources in LDC should benefit themselves and not other countries, and (6) a global commitment to tackle climate change which currently hits LDC the most.

In January 2014, an international conference organized by the International Institute for Environment and Development also discussed priority issues of LDC in the next development agenda.[32] The experts' report identified seven priority issues that need to be recognized in the future. These issues are embedded in a new understanding of genuine partnership between countries, respect for land ownership of LDC, and viewing them as active agents in developing their future and not as victims of past and present circumstances. These priorities include financial aid for development, a global regime of sustainability and equality, good governance, commitment to enhance human and social development, better data and improved productive capacity, dismantling gender inequalities, and tackling climate change issues.

Looking at the various lists of priorities developed, we see a focus on (i) good governance, (ii) human capacity building, (iii) innovation,

---

[30] UN Office of the High Representative for the Least Developed Countries, Landlocked Developing Countries and Small Island Developing States, *Post-2015 Development Agenda: Streamlining Priorities of Least Developed Countries*, unohrlls.org/custom-content/uploads/2013/09/Winter-2012-Commitment1.pdf.

[31] International Institute for Environment and Development, *Taking a Lead on the Post-2015 Agenda: Priorities for Least Developed Countries*, pubs.iied.org/pdfs/17163IIED.pdf.

[32] Roger Williamson and Tom Bigg, *The Post-2015 Development Framework: Priorities for the Least Developed Countries*, pubs.iied.org/pdfs/G03757.pdf.

access to technologies and inclusive economic growth, (iv) financial infrastructure, and (v) ecological measures and climate change management.

We have seen that *Populorum Progressio* can be read as having a soul, a claim for the primacy of the immaterial over the material, the moral over the economic, the inner order over external goods. According to Catholic Social Teaching, human interiority is the basis for an understanding of human dignity: "Man in his interiority transcends the universe and is the only creature willed by God for itself" (*Compendium*, no. 130). Human persons are capable of self-reflection and of a relationship with themselves. "Sacred Scripture speaks in this regard about the heart of man. The heart designates man's inner spirituality" (*Compendium*, no. 114). This understanding of the human person provides a specific perspective on processes of change and transformation: "The inner transformation of the human person, in his being progressively conformed to Christ, is the necessary prerequisite for a real transformation of his relationships with others" (*Compendium*, no. 42).

The first aspect of the task to serve the human person is "*the commitment and efforts to renew oneself interiorly*" (*Compendium*, no. 552). An internal renewal must precede the commitment to improve society. Social change requires change of spiritual attitudes (*Sollicitudo Rei Socialis*, no. 38).

> We are thus invited to re-examine the concept of development. This of course is not limited to merely satisfying material necessities through an increase of goods, while ignoring the sufferings of the many and making the selfishness of individuals and nations the principal motivation. As the Letter of St. James pointedly reminds us: "What causes wars, and what causes fighting among you? Is it not your passions that are at war in your members? You desire and do not have" (*Js* 4:1-2). (*Sollicitudo Rei Socialis*, no. 10)

Inner renewal is the basis for social transformation, starting with the individual person. True development is based on "a lively awareness of the value of the rights of all and of each person" (*Sollicitudo Rei Socialis*, no. 33).

This personalist approach may be at odds with utilitarian macropolicies working with the primacy of efficiency, but this is a consequence of prioritizing the dignity of each human person. *Populorum Progressio* connects the idea of development with personal growth right in the opening paragraph. The Catholic understanding follows less the logic of "It is better for you that one man should die instead of the people, so that the whole nation may not perish" (John 11:50) and more the logic of the lost sheep (Luke 15:4-7) that every single person counts. This very idea sets limits on the criterion of "efficiency" at the core of decision-making processes.

A good example of this logic can be found in the gospel of Luke in the contrast between the temptation "to be spectacular" (Luke 4:9-11) and the Emmaus story (Luke 22) where the risen Lord spends a full day with two individuals rather than demonstrating a spectacular "show for the masses." This alternative logic is an invitation to "slow policies" that attempt to do justice to the individual person, such as Jean Vanier's L'Arche, which helps people to connect with their own vulnerability rather than their efficiency, an experience powerfully described by Henri Nouwen.[33] The principle that every single person counts will justify the special attention to the weakest and the marginalized—the "lost sheep"—rather than helping "the many superficially." This logic seems to suggest a thorough approach to a few with a primacy of depth over breadth. This conviction is part of the personalist basis of Catholic Social Teaching: "the personal development of the members of society ... is the true goal of a nation's economy" (*Mater et Magistra*, no. 74).

The logic of this approach is that no one is left behind, "The truth of development consists in its completeness: if it does not involve the whole man and every man, it is not true development" (*Caritas in Veritate*, no. 19). In order words, authentic development not only affects each person in his or her fullness, it also involves each person. This inclusiveness needs to be vouched for not only in terms of rights but also in terms of responsibilities and duties. Authentic development embraces and engages everyone; each is called to contribute to the development of society as a whole (no. 17).

This commitment to a particular understanding of the human person establishes the primacy of the intangible over the tangible. In his homily at Manger Square, Bethlehem, during his pilgrimage to the Holy Land in May 2009, Pope Benedict exhorted the assembly to cultivate a new spiritual infrastructure: "Your homeland needs not only new economic and community structures, but most importantly, we might say, a new 'spiritual' infrastructure; capable of galvanizing the energies of all men and women of good will in the service of education, development and the promotion of the common good."[34] Spiritual infrastructure could then be said to be the cluster of capabilities to transform reality via spiritual means. Factors contributing to the development of human capabilities may be cultural, social, legal, political or economic in nature and can refer to social cohesion, the levels

[33] Henri Nouwen, *Adam* (New York: Orbis, 2000).
[34] Pope Benedict XVI, "Homily at Manger's Square, Bethlehem," w2.vatican.va/content/benedict-xvi/en/homilies/2009/documents/hf_ben-xvi_hom_20090513_mangiatoia.html.

of political stability, public safety, tax policies, and the strength of institutional frameworks. Alongside the hard factors of tangible infrastructure, the soft factors of intangible infrastructure have to be considered. Spiritual infrastructure is a matter of second order resources, resources that determine our way of utilizing the resources we have at hand. Second-order resources make us ask the questions of how and why and to which purpose to use our first-order resources. This adds an important "telos" component to any discourse on human development.

In the light of these considerations we could now approach the question at stake: According to which priorities should extreme poverty be addressed? The primacy of the "soul" in the light of Catholic Social Teaching would give us the first three priorities focusing on the moral development of citizens, political leaders, and partners from the North and West. The logic behind this ranking of priorities is simple: there can be no sustainable change without a transformation of the inner situation of the key players and the stakeholders involved. Increasing the levels of political participation and strengthening the sense of accountability of those in power will thus also strengthen the sense of ownership and political participation and so must be a priority.[35] Corruption is one of the main impediments to social change; illicit financial flows are responsible for massive losses.[36] There are "enablers" and "beneficiaries" of these flows. There needs to be a shift of focus to the moral fabric of players and stakeholders. The world will not make inroads into eradicating extreme poverty until the most powerful agents accept a strong sense of robust concerns and sincere commitments.[37]

Once a moral and spiritual infrastructure has been established, the most important material resource – finances – can be tackled. Hence, a second set of priorities concerning economic and financial justice, a "good governance" with special regard to the fiscal system and economic opportunities based on a revised debt policy, would seem to be key for the "soul" of Catholic Social Teaching. There must be a clear commitment to pay taxes (*Compendium*, no. 380). Taxes are a key expression of solidarity (no. 355). *Populorum Progressio* explicitly discusses moral aspects of taxation as a major element in development

---

[35] Jennifer Leavy and Joanna Howard, *What Matters Most? Evidence from 84 Participatory Studies with Those Living with Extreme Poverty and Marginalisation* (Sussex, UK: IDS Report, 2015).

[36] See Dev Kar and Devon Cartwright-Smith, *Illicit Financial Flows from Africa: Hidden Resource for Development* (Washington, DC: Global Financial Integrity, 2010).

[37] Else Øyen, "The Paradox of Poverty Research: Why is Extreme Poverty Not in Focus?," in *Absolute Poverty and Global Justice : Empirical Data, Moral Theories, Initiatives*, ed. Elke Mack, Michael Schramm, Stephan Klasen, and Thomas Pogge (Vermont: Ashgate, 2009), 259–271.

efforts (nos. 47, 84). Taxes are the primary concern of domestic policy. In line with the principles of subsidiarity and solidarity, attention must be paid to the fact that anti-poverty policies do have a strong domestic distribution component, are linked to domestic policies, and are not exclusively or even primarily about the transfer of aid.[38] Domestic distribution matters also concern the structures of a welfare state providing for the basic needs of its citizens. No citizen should be forced to live in extreme poverty. However, there is an international level with regard to financial justice as well – the issue of debts. "The right to development must be taken into account when considering questions related to the debt crisis of many poor countries" (*Compendium*, no. 450). A revision of the debt situation can provide ways and means towards real possibilities for states in the South.

The third set of priorities in the light of the "soul" of Catholic Social Teaching is concerned with building local communities by focusing especially on its weakest members. The latter is in line with the preferential option for the poor (or special attention to the weakest members) as an important pillar of Catholic Social Teaching. The weakest members are the children. Hence, this third set of priorities calls for child poverty to be addressed. Child poverty is an obvious priority since children living in extreme poverty will most likely become adults living in chronic poverty. This is an entry point to break the vicious circle. Tackling child poverty is not only about providing moral development and basic infrastructure but also about providing access to proper education and employment.

A particular element of combating child poverty is the strengthening of families. A well-established element of Catholic Social Teaching is the claim that the family is the basis of social and political life and that the family as the first school of life prepares children for future citizenship (*Compendium*, no. 210ff). This is the relevance of the family for macro-structures (*Gaudium et Spes*, nos. 36, 48). The macro-structures are called to protect and sustain the family, including the payment of wages that make it possible for a family to support itself (*Rerum Novarum*, no. 13; *Quadragesima Anno*, no. 71; *Centesimus Annus*, no. 8). Poor families have poor children. Poor children suffer most and are the most vulnerable. They develop the above mentioned "mental landscapes," "mind[s] shaped by poverty."[39]

---

[38] Andy Sumner, "Poverty, Politics and Aid: Is a Reframing of Global Poverty Approaching?," *Third World Quarterly* 34, no. 3 (2013): 357-377.

[39] See Regenia Rawlinson, *A Mind Shaped By Poverty* (Indiana: I-Universe, 2011). Rawlinson describes the result of a childhood in poverty as a particular mindset: feelings of powerlessness, self-sabotage, the attitude that one has to fight for everything.

The commitment to weaker persons and contexts can also be translated into geographies. Weaker regions can be understood to be an expression of the principle of subsidiarity and the implications of the insight that location is a main factor in poverty traps, especially when we face households located in remote areas.[40] Rural development, strengthening grass roots communities, and community building have been recognized as salient factors in fighting poverty.[41] This is also a strategy which could be employed to counter hyper-urbanization. A crucial component in strengthening local communities is the building of proper local governance according to "good local governance" schemes following a common good orientation and avoiding corruption, bureaucratization, and the "Tragedy of the Commons."

A fourth set of priorities suggests measures be introduced to build an inclusive economy: to provide work opportunities and employment possibilities for women, to afford access to new technologies and to make incentives available for innovation. A final priority must be ecology. The environment has already been discussed as a development challenge in *Octogesima Adveniens*, no. 21. The emphasis on ecology and the preferential option for the poor are not disconnected. There are complex links between climate change and poverty, as *Laudato Si'* explicitly states (nos. 13, 16, 20, 25).[42] Fighting poverty and caring for creation go hand in hand, they cannot be separated.

CONCLUSION

A Catholic understanding of development, based on a certain reading of Catholic Social Teaching documents, especially of *Populorum Progressio*, underlines the primacy of the immaterial over the material dimension of development; immaterial goods such as desires and ideas take priority. Thus, one can view Catholic Social teaching as having a "soul," and this "soul" plays a major role in development work. If one were to take this "primacy of the inner" seriously, one could identify priorities of development planning on the macro-level. The fact that Pope Francis established a new dicastery for the promotion of integral human development is an invitation to accept the close link between spirituality and development. This provides hope, a hope beautifully expressed in *Populorum Progressio*, no. 17 in an image that expresses

---

[40] Akhter Ahmed, Ruth Vargas Hill, Lisa Smith, Doris Wiesmann, and Tim Frankenberger, *The World's Most Deprived: Characteristics and Causes of Extreme Poverty and Hunger* (Washington, DC: International Food Policy Research Institute, 2007).

[41] Stephen C. Smith, *Ending Global Poverty: A Guide that Works* (Basingstoke, UK: Palgrave Macmillan, 2005).

[42] See Robin Leichenko and Julie Silva, "Climate Change and Poverty: Vulnerability, Impacts, and Alleviation Strategies: Climate Change and Poverty," *Wiley Interdisciplinary Reviews: Climate Change* 5, no. 4 (2014): 539–556.

the trust in God who works in history: "As the waves of the sea gradually creep farther and farther in along the shoreline, so the human race inches its way forward through history."■

Journal of Moral Theology, Vol. 6, No. 1 (2017): 39-56

The Justice Legacy of *Populorum Progressio*: a Jesuit Case Study

Kevin Ahern

OVER THE PAST FIVE DECADES since the 1967 publication of *Populorum Progressio*, Roman Catholic organizations have taken leadership roles in some of the most important efforts for social change around the world. From the work of the "Nuns on the Bus" for economic justice reform in the United States to the efforts of Catholic organizations against authoritarian regimes during the "third wave of democracy" in Brazil, Poland, and the Philippines, many Catholic groups, inspired by the Gospel and Catholic social teaching, have become active agents in transforming social and political structures.[1]

For many religious congregations and lay movements, this public commitment to justice, development, and social transformation owes much to the integral framework proposed by Pope Paul VI in *Populorum Progressio*. As the first social encyclical written after the Second Vatican Council, the 1967 document offers an application of conciliar doctrine to a global context marked increasingly by the power of transnational structures and systems. In the text, the pope outlines the church's "global vision" of what it means to be human by drawing attention to the complex nature of each person and society. Authentic development, he famously insisted, "cannot be limited to mere economic growth…it must be complete: integral, that is, it has to promote the good of every man and of the whole man" (no. 14).

Populorum Progressio's impact, however, goes beyond its teachings on development. It also widens an understanding of the church's mission and its relationship to the world to include direct action for social transformation. This integral framework, which was developed further in *Octogesima Adveniens, Justice in the World*, and *Evangelii Nuntiandi*, profoundly impacted the way church communities perceived their role in the world. Inspired by this integral model, many Catholic organizations, including lay movements and religious con-

---

[1] See Kevin Ahern, *Structures of Grace: Catholic Organizations Serving the Global Common Good* (New York: Orbis Books, 2015).

gregations, including the Society of Jesus, redefined their own missions to include action for integral human development and social justice.

The missiological turn to social justice emerging from *Populorum Progressio*, however, was not welcome by all in the church. Other models of mission, for example, downplay the church's direct role in social transformation, leading to contentious debates of how best to address a context marked by social and structural sin. What, then, is the proper role of the church and church organizations in regards to social justice?

This paper examines this question in light of the social justice legacy of *Populorum Progressio* in three steps. Part I will consider the work of the Jesuit Refugee Service, a major Catholic organization that embodies Paul VI's integral model in its work with forcibly displaced people around the world. Part II will then consider this experience considering the two major post-conciliar models of mission, starting with the integral framework presented in *Populorum Progressio*. Finally, this paper concludes by briefly examining the legacy of Paul's integral model in the papacy of Pope Francis, the first Jesuit pope, who both develops and expands the model offered by *Populorum Progressio*.

ACTION FOR JUSTICE AT THE MARGINS:
JESUIT REFUGEE SERVICE

The Jesuit Refugee Service (JRS) has witnessed to God's merciful love to some of the most marginalized of human beings since its foundation in 1980 by Pedro Arrupe, SJ. As a modest switchboard of coordination, JRS has grown to be one of the most innovative humanitarian agencies in the world. Presently, over 900,000 people in more than 50 countries are directly served by an international staff of 1,400, including 78 Jesuits and 66 members of other religious congregations.[2] JRS additionally employs thousands of others in the local communities in which they work.

The work of JRS goes beyond charitable efforts in refugee communities. At the international level, JRS acts as a voice for social and political change through its status as a nongovernmental organization (NGO) with the United Nations system. Through this official accreditation, it lobbies governments and seeks to raise public awareness to the plight of the millions of forcibly displaced women, men, and children around the world.

Rooted in the Jesuit tradition and Ignatian spirituality, JRS's mission at both the centers of political power and at the margins of society is threefold: to "accompany, serve and defend the rights of refugees

---

[2] Jesuit Refugee Service, "Who We Are: About Us," en.jrs.net/about.

and forcibly displaced people."[3] This mission, as the next section shows, developed out of the integral framework embodied in *Populorum Progressio* and the renewed articulation of the Jesuit mission in the 1970s. A discussion of the work of JRS requires that we first examine what this threefold mission looks like in practice and also consider where action for justice enters the equation.

Accompaniment

More than anything perhaps, JRS is defined by the Ignatian principle of accompaniment, which according to its Charter is the task of affirming to refugees "that God is present in human history, even in most tragic episodes."[4] In many respects, this is the organization's hallmark. In a world where many humanitarian actors maintain a professional distance from the people they serve, JRS's "style of presence" makes it unique.[5] In this way, the apostolic work of JRS goes deeper than simply providing urgently needed material relief and advocacy. True to its etymological roots, the Jesuit practice of accompaniment can literally involve "breaking bread" with those in need. Reflecting *Populorum Progressio*'s commitment to the development of the whole person, JRS seeks to be attentive to the multifaceted nature of the women and men that it serves, including their social, physical, spiritual, and physiological needs.[6] For those facing a desperate reality far from home, the presence of a compassionate companion can engender hope and contribute to healing following a trauma.[7] In many places, JRS is the only agency to offer spiritual and psychological support through counseling, prayer, the sacraments, and community building.[8] For example, JRS USA's Detention Chaplaincy Program offers pastoral care for detained migrants of all faiths in government detention centers. Chaplains and volunteers celebrate Mass, lead ecu-

---

[3] Jesuit Refugee Service, "The Charter of Jesuit Refugee Service," no. 9, en.jrs.net/assets/Sections/Downloads/char-en2.pdf.

[4] Jesuit Refugee Service, "The Charter of Jesuit Refugee Service," no. 15.

[5] See Daniel Villanueva, "The Jesuit Way of Going Global: Outlines for a Public Presence of the Society of Jesus in a Globalized World in the Light of Lessons Learned from the Jesuit Refugee Service," (STL Thesis, Weston Jesuit School of Theology, 2008), 79; Pablo Alonso et al., eds., *God in Exile: Towards a Shared Spirituality with Refugees* (Rome: Jesuit Refugee Service, 2005), chap. 2.

[6] Mark Raper, "Pastoral Accompaniment Among Refugees: The Jesuit Refugee Service Experience," in *Everybody's Challenge: Essential Documents of Jesuit Refugee Service, 1980-2000*, ed. Danielle Vella (Rome: Jesuit Refugee Service, 2000), 84.

[7] Michael J. Schultheis, "Rebuilding the Bridges and Clearing the Footpaths: A Parable of JRS," in *The Wound of the Border: 25 Years With the Refugees*, ed. Amaya Valcárcel (Rome: Jesuit Refugee Service, 2005), 146.

[8] Raper, "Pastoral Accompaniment Among Refugees," 87–88.

menical prayer services, facilitate fellowship, and offer spiritual counseling. In 2005 alone, JRS coordinated over 2,000 religious services
at detention centers throughout the United States.[9]

Service

As with other humanitarian aid organizations, JRS offers essential
humanitarian services to people who have been forcibly displaced, including legal assistance, medical care and nutrition. As such, it lives
out the corporal works of mercy in a profound way through its service
to refugee populations by responding to the needs of those who are
hungry, thirsty, ill, impoverished, dead, diseased, imprisoned, and
without homes. The two primary areas of service for JRS are education and psychosocial/pastoral care. Both are a natural fit for a work
of the Society of Jesus. Indeed, it is one of the few organizations to
offer educational projects to refugees in camps and urban centers, including an innovative effort to provide access to higher education
through online distance learning.[10]

Advocacy and Justice

For JRS, accompaniment and direct service give rise to a commitment to advocate on behalf of and defend the forcibly displaced. At its
core, this task seeks to go beyond providing temporary relief of suffering to address the root causes of forced displacement. Locally, advocacy could mean addressing specific concerns with refugee camp
officials or advocating on behalf of a person with governments or
other humanitarian agencies. At the national and international level,
JRS's commitment to defend the rights of forcibly displaced persons
leads it to address both the root causes of forced displacement and the
political and humanitarian responses to the movements of people
across borders. These efforts do not aspire to be a temporary solution
for humanitarian conflicts; "rather they aim at healing the wounds of
exile. Above all, they seek to prevent fresh wounds."[11] Whenever possible, JRS seeks to empower refugees to speak on their own behalf,
accompanying them as they bring their experiences to those in power.
Consider, for instance, the role of JRS in the International Campaign to Ban Landmines.[12] Disturbed by the horrific wounds of many

---

[9] Jesuit Refugee Service USA, "Detention Chaplaincy Program," jrsusa.org/cam-
paigns_focus?TN=PROMO-20100907030248.
[10] See "Jesuit Commons: Higher Education at the Margins," 2016, www.jc-hem.org.
[11] Christophe Renders, "Speak Out, Judge Righteously, Defend the Rights of the
Poor and Needy (Pr 31: 9)," in *God in Exile: Towards a Shared Spirituality with
Refugees*, Pablo Alonso et al., eds., (Rome: Jesuit Refugee Service, 2005), 107
[12] Mark Raper, "Mercy and the National Interest," in *Everybody's Challenge: Essential Documents of Jesuit Refugee Service, 1980-2000*, ed. Danielle Vella (Rome: Jesuit Refugee Service, 2000), 65; Amaya Valcárcel and Danielle Vella, eds., *Advocacy
in Jesuit Refugee Service* (Rome: Jesuit Refugee Service, 2011), 23.

refugees from landmines, JRS staff in Cambodia and other countries mobilized the global Jesuit network to analyze the root causes and propose lasting alternatives. JRS's role in the international campaign has greatly reduced the use of landmines, a significant change for those forced to cross borders.[13] In other words, JRS's work is not limited only to charity or the humanitarian manifestations of the corporal works of mercy. Rather, its service and accompaniment with refugees leads it to work to transform some of the social structures that are at the root of their suffering. For JRS and other Jesuit endeavors involved in advocacy work today, efforts aimed at transforming social structures are grounded in a specific reading of Ignatian spirituality and Christian discipleship.[14] Peter Hans Kolvenbach, SJ, the former Father General of the Jesuits, summarizes the importance of justice this way:

> The Church discovered only very slowly that charity is not sufficient if there is no justice. What has to be done by JRS is not just charity but also justice. If you really love, you will do justice. You will not do justice out of justice, but out of love… it is very clear all these people have their rights, which need to be attended to. They have the right to go back to their country. They have the right to join in a just society. JRS is called to help do this, not out of legal or juridical motivations but out of Christian love.[15]

In this commitment to both charity and justice, JRS is not unique among Catholic organizations. In the wake of the Second Vatican Council and *Populorum Progressio*, many ecclesial communities came to see action for social justice and transformation to be core elements of their own specific missions. For example, well over a hundred Catholic NGOs, including religious congregations, church agencies, and lay movements, have formal nongovernmental consultative status with the United Nations or specific UN agencies. These include several Jesuit-related organizations such as Fe y Alegria, Center of Concern, the International Jesuit Network for Development, Jesuit European Office-OCIPE, the Indian Social Institute, the World Christian Life Community and several congregations of women religious with an Ignatian charism. Like JRS, these organizations make use of their accreditation to actively lobby governments and intergovernmental or-

---

[13] David Hollenbach, "The Jesuits and the 'More Universal Good': At Vatican II and Today," in *The Jesuits and Globalization: Historical Legacies and Contemporary Challenges*, ed. José Casanova and Thomas Banchoff (Washington, DC: Georgetown University Press, 2016), 181.

[14] In "A Model of Ignatian Advocacy," *Promotio Justitiae* 101, no. 1 (2009): 40, Frank Turner of the Jesuit European Office defines Ignatian advocacy as being "spiritual, attentive to deep feeling, intellectual, [and] oriented to action."

[15] Peter-Hans Kolvenbach, "Address," Presented at the Jesuit Refugee Service International Meeting, Santa Severa, Italy, 2006.

ganizations on issues of social concern. It is not uncommon, for example, to see sisters, priests, and lay leaders presenting statements calling for changes in international policy and law at major meetings of the United Nations.[16]

ACTION FOR JUSTICE AND THE CHURCH'S MISSION IN THE WORLD

Not everyone appreciates the direct public action for social justice by Catholic organizations and their convictions that transforming society is part of their religious mission. For the so-called "new atheists" and the champions of laïcité style secularism, there is simply no room for any religious agent in the public sphere. Religion, as some argue, "poisons everything."[17] For others, advocacy and the promotion of justice by any refugee-serving NGO is perceived as violating the traditional humanitarian principles of impartiality, neutrality, and independence first articulated by Jean Pictet, the founder of the International Committee of the Red Cross.[18] Proponents of this approach believe these values are the most effective ways to create a protective "space" to serve the immediate needs of refugees. Advocacy, long-term strategies for development, and attention to human rights are seen as too political and thus in violation of humanitarianism's sacred principles.[19]

The resistance to the work of JRS and other Catholic organizations for justice also comes from within the church. Some theologians, church leaders, and Jesuits themselves have argued that it is simply not the role of church institutions, particularly those of priests and religious, to be directly involved in struggles for political, social and economic change. In order to fully appreciate the impact of *Populorum Progressio* on Catholic organizational life, it is helpful to examine how corporate action for justice relates to three different models of mission that took shape in the twentieth century.

---

[16] See Kevin Ahern, "Mediating the Global Common Good: Catholic NGOs and the Future of Global Governance," in *Public Theology and the Global Common Good: Essays in Honor of David Hollenbach*, ed. Kristin E. Heyer et al. (New York: Orbis Books, 2016), 14-25; Emeka Obiezu, Joan F. Burke, and Cecile Meijer, eds., *It Is Good for Us to Be Here: Catholic Religious Institutes as NGOs at the United Nations* (Indiana: Xlibris LCC, 2015).

[17] Christopher Hitchens, *God Is Not Great: How Religion Poisons Everything* (New York: Twelve, 2007).

[18] Legitimate questions can be raised as to the feasibility of maintaining a neutral stance in conflict situations. See, for example, the critique of the ICRC in the face of the Holocaust in Jean-Claude Favez, *The Red Cross and the Holocaust* (Cambridge: Cambridge University Press, 1999).

[19] See David Rieff, *A Bed for the Night: Humanitarianism in Crisis* (New York: Simon & Schuster, 2002); Michael N. Barnett and Thomas G. Weiss, eds., *Humanitarianism in Question: Politics, Power, Ethics* (Ithaca, NY: Cornell University, 2008).

Educators, not Actors, for Justice: The Distinction of Planes

In the lead-up to the Second Vatican Council, French Catholic thinkers, particularly Jacques Maritain and Yves Congar, OP, outlined a new approach to the church/world relationship. Responding to the limits of the Christendom model, which sought to place society under the control of clerical church leaders, these thinkers proposed the "distinction of planes" framework. Here, clear delineations are made between the church and the temporal plane, between the responsibilities of the church and those of the laity, and between the actions of a Christian and the actions of a Christian as such.[20]

The laity, inspired by church teachings, are called to act as Christians in the temporal plane as they seek to transform society. But this is done in a personal capacity. By contrast, the actions of Christians as such, in which the believer participates in the church's mission, takes place only within the ecclesial-liturgical plane of action and, when necessary, to defend the church's interests in the world.[21]

Such a framework leaves little room for the work of JRS and other ecclesial efforts for social transformation. Church organizations, especially those of priests and vowed religious, are limited to a spiritual and pedagogical sphere. For example, it is not the role of Catholic lay movements or congregations, as organizations, Congar wrote, to take up "the task of the direct 'technical transformation of the political or economic structures.'"[22] Rather, their role is limited to "prepare laymen to act as Christians" in the worldly plane.[23]

Populorum Progressio: *Integrating Justice and Mission*

With the Second Vatican Council, a new model of mission begins to emerge that erodes the rigid distinctions between the church and the world and between the laity and the church. In *Lumen Gentium*, for example, the council speaks of the responsibility of the whole church, "the people of God," to be a "sign and instrument" of God's salvific love in history (nos. 1 and 9). In a similar vein, *Ad Gentes* reframes mission by affirming the call of all the baptized to participate in mission (no. 35). Both *Apostolicam Actuositatem* (nos. 19-23) and *Gaudium et Spes* (no. 90) specifically affirm the social action of Catholic organizations at the international level. At the same time, however, other conciliar passages support the distinction of planes model by suggesting that it is the "special vocation" of the laity, and not the

---

[20] See Gustavo Gutiérrez, *A Theology of Liberation: History, Politics, and Salvation* (New York: Orbis Books, 1988), 36–38.

[21] Jacques Maritain, *Integral Humanism: Temporal and Spiritual Problems of a New Christendom*, trans. Joseph W. Evans (New York: Scribner and Sons, 1968), 294 and 269.

[22] Yves Congar, *Lay People in the Church: A Study for a Theology of Laity*, trans. Donald Attwater (Maryland: Newman, 1956), 269.

[23] Maritain, *Integral Humanism*, 298.

church as a whole, to engage the temporal sphere (*Apostolicam Actuositatem*, nos. 2 and 4). In many ways, it is these ambiguities in the conciliar texts that have allowed for the development of two different post-conciliar models of mission.

One of these approaches begins to takes shape with *Populorum Progressio*. Here, Paul VI's global vision of the person and society offers a redefinition of both development and mission. According to this model, which Stephen Bevans and Roger Schroeder describe as "liberating service of the reign of God," there are clear links between the church's mission, human development, liberation, and the transformation of social structures.[24] Applying the council's "renewed consciousness" to the topic of development, the encyclical offers three important insights that help to frame this new understanding of how the church and church organizations should relate to the world.

First, drawing on the council's renewed attention to scripture and the Christological grounding employed by *Gaudium et Spes*, *Populorum Progressio* links concern for human development and the plight of those in poverty directly with the mission entrusted to the church by Christ. While it recognizes the different roles played by the church and the state, the encyclical points to Jesus Christ to affirm the church's role and responsibility in the world (no. 13). Indeed, the "teaching and example" of Christ, "who cited the preaching of the Gospel to the poor as a sign of His mission" inspires the church to "foster the human progress of the nations to which she brings faith in Christ" (no. 12).

Toward the end of the document, we see that Paul is aware that such a mission with such a strong social concern is not easy, as it "certainly calls for hard work and imposes difficult sacrifices" (no. 79). This is something that many JRS staff know well as they make the choice to accompany those in dangerous and desperate places. For Paul, the difficulties experienced in bringing about a more fully human development unite oneself to the sacrifice of Christ on the cross.

Second, *Populorum Progressio* offers an important "integral" vision of what it means to flourish as a person and as a society. Building upon the work of the French Dominican theologian Louis-Joseph Lebret, two key aspects of "integral human development" are identified. On the one hand, it encourages concern for the development of all persons in a world divided by nationalism, racism, and individualism. The reality of human solidarity and our shared membership in the one human family calls us to "build a human community where [all people] can live truly human lives" (no. 47).

---

[24] See Stephen B. Bevans and Roger Schroeder, *Constants in Context: A Theology of Mission for Today* (New York: Orbis Books, 2004), chapter 10.

At the same time, Paul VI's framework seeks to promote the development of the whole person, including their spiritual, social, physical, and economic dimensions (no. 14). Human development, therefore, cannot be seen in merely technical or economic terms, nor can it be separated from questions of justice and peace. Such a framework has much to say to Christians about their relationship to the world. A holistic anthropology makes it difficult to sharply separate the "spiritual" and "temporal" planes of existence.[25] Authentic work for development, which includes attention to social justice, and spiritual development are, thus, deeply connected to one another (no. 76).

Finally, with this integral approach to development and its corresponding integral vision of mission, there is an awareness that charitable efforts alone are insufficient for the church to assist in the promotion of development. The second section of *Populorum Progressio* highlights the ways in which missionaries, inspired by the example of Jesus, have contributed to social development throughout history. Here, one can think of the many schools, hospitals, and apostolic works built by missionary congregations, including the Jesuits. Though, as he points out, they might not always have been perfect in their projects, the pope commends the work of these pioneers in responding to the social and cultural needs of people (no. 12). Given the growing global interdependence and complexities of the problems facing the human family, such local and individual efforts, he writes, are "no longer enough." The problems facing people today demand more than charitable works. Paul VI points to the need for "concerted effort of everyone," and "a thorough examination of every facet of the problem—social, economic, cultural and spiritual" (no. 13). Near the end of the document, the pope calls upon all Catholics in "developed nations to offer their skills and earnest assistance to public and private organizations, both civil and religious" to work for change, including the establishment of "just and fair laws, based on moral precepts, established among all nations" (no. 81).

The holistic vision of *Populorum Progressio* and its attention to the systematic and structural dimensions of poverty go a long way to help frame the justice work of organizations such as the Jesuit Refugee Service.[26] This integral vision of human development and mission is developed in substantial ways over the following decade in Pope Paul's subsequent teachings as well as by groups of bishops, theologians, and Catholic lay movements and religious congregations. A few

---

[25] See Dean Brackley, *Divine Revolution: Salvation and Liberation in Catholic Thought* (New York: Orbis Books, 1996).

[26] See "The Statutes of JRS as a Foundation of Canonical Rite" (Jesuit Refugee Service, 2003), Art. 7, for JRS' articulation of its mission: "The mission of JRS is to take care of the pastoral needs of the refugees and their religious and spiritual formation. JRS also attend to their human, spiritual, material and cultural needs and defends their human rights."

months after the release of the text, for example, eighteen bishops from ten countries, under the leadership of Archbishop Hélder Câmara of Brazil, responded positively to the encyclical in their "Letter to the Peoples of the Third World."[27]

The encyclical features prominently, for example, in Gustavo Gutiérrez's seminal presentation, "Toward a Theology of Liberation" of 1968. In that text, Gutiérrez praises the "theological progress" made by *Populorum Progressio* as he links integral development, liberation, and salvation.[28] That same year, a group of Jesuit provincials issued a statement on "the Jesuits in Latin America," in which they call upon Jesuits in the region to "work for the liberation of humankind from every sort of servitude that oppresses it."[29] This reading of *Populorum Progressio* within the context of Latin America can also be seen in the documents issued by the Second General Conference of Latin American Bishops in Medellín, which cite the encyclical repeatedly.

Building on the reception of *Populorum Progressio* around the world, several important documents issued in 1971 highlight the church's growing social justice consciousness. Pope Paul's apostolic letter *Octogesima Adveniens* offers one of the most sustained calls for the church to take "effective action" against injustices in the world (no. 48). Here, Catholic organizations are mentioned explicitly as playing an important role in this regard (no. 51). This same point is repeated in two separate documents issued soon after *Octogesima Adveniens*. The Vatican's *Guidelines for the Definition of Catholic International Organizations* clearly identifies the public engagement of international Catholic lay organizations at United Nations as participating "in the mission of the Church."[30] At the same time, *Evangelica Testificatio*, the apostolic exhortation on the renewal of religious life, affirms the role of religious "in the sphere of works of mercy, assistance and social justice" (no. 16).

The most influential statement on this matter appears later in 1971, from the World Synod of Bishops. In their final statement, *Justice in the World*, the bishops root the church's vocation to act for justice in God's Reign and the Gospel demands to love one's neighbor. The

---

[27] Third World Bishops, "A Letter to the Peoples of the Third World (August 15, 1967)," in *Liberation Theology: A Documentary History*, ed. Alfred T. Hennelly (New York: Orbis Books, 1990), 48–57.

[28] Gustavo Gutiérrez, "Toward a Theology of Liberation (July, 1968)," in *Liberation Theology: A Documentary History*, ed. Alfred T. Hennelly (New York: Orbis Books, 1990), 69–71.

[29] Provincial of the Society of Jesus, "The Jesuits in Latin America (May 1968)," in *Liberation Theology: A Documentary History*, ed. Alfred T. Hennelly (New York: Orbis Books, 1990), 78.

[30] Pontifical Council for the Laity, "Respiciens Normas Quibus Instituta Internationalia Catholica Definiuntur," *Acta Apostolicae Sedis* 63, no. 1 (1971): 952.

Synod's most influential and controversial sentence appears in its in-
troductory section with the claim that "action on behalf of justice and
participation in the transformation of the world is a constitutive dimension" of the "Church's mission."[31]

This paragraph was a point of contention at the subsequent 1974
Synod, meeting on the theme of evangelization.[32] In particular, questions were raised concerning the most appropriate way to interpret
"constitutive." Is action for justice so essential, some asked, that there
could be no evangelization without it? Responding to these debates,
Paul VI's post-apostolic exhortation *Evangelii Nuntiandi*, issued a
year after the Synod, points to evangelization—not action for justice—as the "constitutive" element of the church's mission (no. 160).
This does not mean, however, that justice is foreign to mission. Indeed, expanding on *Populorum Progressio*'s integral framework,
Evangelii Nuntiandi envisions mission as a "complex process made
up of varied elements: the renewal of humanity, witness, explicit proclamation, inner adherence, entry into the community, acceptance of
signs, apostolic initiative" (no. 24).

Mindful of the dangers of reducing "mission to the dimensions of
a simply temporal project"—what has been called "horizontalism"—
Paul prioritizes Christ's message of liberation from sin. However,
Christ's great gift of salvation is not just spiritual, as it involves a "liberation from everything that oppresses" people (no. 9). Indeed, evangelization and the spreading of the Good News would be "incom-
plete," he argues, if it fails to consider "the unceasing interplay of the
Gospel and of [a person's] concrete life, both personal and social" (no.
29).

Populorum Progressio and the Jesuit Mission

The shift toward a more holistic model of mission, which differed
from the preconciliar distinction of planes model, had a significant impact on the Jesuit understanding of mission. Like many religious orders, the Society of Jesus redefined its mission in this period following
the council's call for the renewal of religious life. The key figure in
the Jesuit renewal was Pedro Arrupe, who participated in both the
1971 and 1974 synods in his capacity as the father general of the Society of Jesus. Through his leadership, the 32nd General Congregation
of the Society of Jesus (1974-1975) reflects this framework as it profoundly rearticulated the Jesuit mission in its famous "Decree Four:

---

[31] Synod of Bishops, *"Justitia in Mundo*, Justice in the World (1971)," in *Catholic
Social Thought: The Documentary Heritage*, ed. David J. O'Brien and Thomas A.
Shannon (New York: Orbis Books, 2010).

[32] Charles M. Murphy, "Action for Justice as Constitutive of the Preaching of the
Gospel: What Did the 1971 Synod Mean?," in *Readings in Moral Theology, No. 5:
Official Catholic Social Teaching*, ed. Charles E. Curran and Richard A. McCor-
mick (New York: Paulist Press, 1986), 160.

Our Mission Today." Echoing the integral model used by *Populorum Progressio*, the 1968 meeting of Jesuit provincials in Latin America, and the debates at the 1971 and 1974 Synods, the document states "the mission of the Society of Jesus today is the service of faith, of which the promotion of justice is an absolute requirement. For reconciliation with God demands the reconciliation of people with one another."[33] The wording of this decree – embedding justice in the Society's mission – as Thomas Greene, SJ reflects, "has become part and parcel of our Jesuit response when we are asked to define the contemporary mission of the Society."[34] It is also, not surprisingly, at the heart of the organization founded by Arrupe, the Jesuit Refugee Service, which cites this section from "Decree Four" in its Charter.

The turn to justice by the Jesuits and other Catholic organizations was not always easy. For many Catholic organizations, the turn to this holistic model of mission resulted in sacrifices and difficulties, like the ones that Paul VI warns about at the end of *Populorum Progressio* (no. 79). Among Jesuits, for example, more than 50 priests and brothers have been killed since the 32nd General Congregation because of their work among the poor. Many of these, like the Martyrs of the University of Central America in San Salvador (El Salvador), were specifically targeted for assassination because their embodiments of mission were seen as a threat to the political or economic order.

Admittedly, sometimes this was not always done in a balanced and thoughtful way. In some areas, efforts to implement the new orientations were done hastily and resulted in confusion and conflict.[35] In other cases, the spiritual and religious dimensions of this integral model were lost as some lay and religious organizations focused all of their energy on the social or horizontal dimensions of evangelization.

The New Evangelization: A Return to the Distinction of Planes?

Partly as a response to these excesses in the church's turn to social justice, a different missiological framework took shape during the pontificates of John Paul II and Benedict XVI. Here, concerns are raised about the dangers of reducing mission only to its horizontal and social dimensions. According to this "new evangelization" approach,

---

[33] General Congregation 32, "Decree 4: Our Mission Today: The Service of Faith and the Promotion of Justice," in *Jesuit Life and Mission Today: The Decrees of the 31st-35th General Congregations of the Society of Jesus*, ed. John W. Padberg, Jesuit Primary Sources in English Translation 25 (Missouri: Institute of Jesuit Sources, 2009), 2.

[34] Tom Greene, "Observations of the Social Apostolate, Justice and the Decrees of General Congregations 31 to 35," *Promotio Justitiae*, 108, no. 1 (2012): 6.

[35] Maria Clara Lucchetti Bingemer, "The Jesuits and Social Justice in Latin America," in *The Jesuits and Globalization: Historical Legacies and Contemporary Challenges*, ed. José Casanova and Thomas Banchoff (Washington, DC: Georgetown University Press, 2016), 188–205.

the fundamental task of the church is not to transform social structures but to proclaim Jesus Christ to an increasingly secularized culture and to witness to God's love though acts of charity.

The change of tone is evident in *Sollicitudo Rei Socialis*, John Paul II's encyclical commemorating the anniversary of *Populorum Progressio*. While it offers a valuable reading of Paul's teaching on global development and strongly highlights the responsibility of Christians to work for solidarity, the text downplays the role of the church and Catholic organizations. Rather than describing the church as an agent for justice, John Paul II speaks of its role in terms of "guiding people's behavior" and giving rise to personal "commitments to justice" (no. 41). This indirect approach, as Mary Elsbrand points out, amounts to a "reinterpretation" of Paul VI's teaching for collective social action, particularly in *Octogesima Adveniens*. Much like the distinction of planes model, the church's role, according to John Paul II, ought to be limited to educating and inspiring personal action.

Redemptoris Missio develops this line of thought as it laments the reduction of salvation to its "horizontal dimension" among certain missionary groups in the church (nos. 2 and 59). The priority of mission should be the proclamation of Jesus Christ and the salvation from sin. This, he argues, cannot be put aside by those involved in social action or dialogue. A decade later, the Congregation for the Doctrine of the Faith, under the leadership of Joseph Ratzinger, argued this point in *Dominus Iesus*.

Not surprisingly, Benedict XVI largely follows the line of his predecessor. In *Deus Caritas Est*, he speaks of charity, and not justice, as the constitutive element in the church's mission (nos. 20-25).[36] Here, he highlights the distinct roles of the church and the state, charity and justice, the laity and the church. It is the role of the state, not the church, he writes, to safeguard and promote justice. The church does not seek a direct engagement in political questions, but instead aims to "purify reason" through its social doctrine (no. 28). Much like the distinction of planes model, Benedict stresses that the lay faithful "are called to take part in public life in a personal capacity" (no. 29). In his 2007 address to the leadership of more than eighty Catholic nongovernmental organizations working with the United Nations, Benedict cites this section of *Deus Caritas Est* when describing the role played by what the Vatican describes as Catholic inspired NGOs, rather than

---

[36] See also Charles M. Murphy, "Charity, Not Justice, as Constitutive of the Church's Mission," *Theological Studies* 68, no. 2 (2007): 274–286.

the long established language of international Catholic organizations.[37]

"The unavoidable connotation" with this line of thought, as Lisa Sowle Cahill points out, is that "the 'real' church consists in the hierarchy, with the laity serving an auxiliary role."[38] For many ecclesial movements, this distinction between direct and indirect social action is problematic because it opposes their collective actions for justice with their ecclesial identity. The final sections of *Deus Caritas Est*, in fact, warns the church's charitable and humanitarian organizations, like JRS, not to be "inspired by ideologies aimed at improving the world" (no. 33).

Concern over "horizontalism" among ecclesial movements is strongly developed a few months later. Citing *Redemptoris Missio* and *Deus Caritas Est*, the Congregation of the Doctrine of the Faith's *Doctrinal Note on Some Aspects of Evangelization* raises concerns with what it perceives as relativistic or reductionist forms of evangelization, especially in the areas of social action and dialogue (no. 3). Nowhere in the *Note* do we see the teaching of Paul VI that action for social justice in the world is an integral part of evangelization.

With *Caritas in Veritate*, however, there are signs of what Cahill describes as a "political reorientation" in Benedict's understanding of this question as he looks to the teachings of *Populorum Progressio*.[39] While he still prioritizes the role of social doctrine in the formation of conscience, he acknowledges in *Caritas in Veritate* that "testimony to Christ's charity, through works of justice, peace, and development, is part and parcel of evangelization" (no. 15). This is an important movement in Benedict's thought that clearly supports the public engagement of church organizations. But this is largely lost in the subsequent post-synodal apostolic exhortation *Africae Munus* and the preparation documents leading up to the Synod on the New Evangelization in 2012. Collective action for justice and the role of Christian organizations, in fact, factors very little in the official texts of the 2012 synod, a fact noted by a few of the participants, including one bishop who critiqued the synod's document for being "rather weak" in its treatment of justice.[40]

---

[37] Benedict XVI, "Address of His Holiness Benedict XVI to Representatives of the Holy See, to International Organizations and to Participants in the Forum of Catholic-Inspired Non-Governmental Organizations," w2.vatican.va/content/benedict-xvi/en/speeches/2007/december/documents/hf_ben-xvi_spe_20071201_ong.html.

[38] Lisa Sowle Cahill, "*Caritas in Veritate*: Benedict's Global Reorientation," *Theological Studies* 71, no. 2 (2010): 297.

[39] Cahill, "*Caritas in Veritate*," 304.

[40] "Intervention of H. Exc. Rev. Mons. François Lapierre, P. M. E., Bishop of Saint-Hyacinthe (Canada)," *Synodus Episcoporum Bollettino*, no. 12 (October 13, 2012), www.vatican.va/news_services/press/sinodo/documents/bollettino_25_xiii-ordinaria-2012/02_inglese/b14_02.html.

The New Evangelization and the Jesuit Mission

Similar debates over which model of mission is appropriate can also be seen within the Society of Jesus. In a dialogue between David Hollenbach, SJ, and Avery Dulles, SJ, for example, Dulles expressed concerns that the justice focus of "Decree Four" would overshadow and diminish the mission of the Society and the role of Jesuits both as scholars and as priests.[41] In his 1994 book, *Faith Beyond Justice: Widening the Perspective*, Martin Tripole, SJ, offers one of the most extensive critiques of 32nd General Congregation's formulation of the Jesuit mission. Reflecting many of the concerns of the new evangelization model, Tripole argues that the promotion of justice had been "raised by GC 32 to an inappropriate level of foundational mission principle."[42] While the promotion of justice, he admits, may be a legitimate response to the charism of St. Ignatius today, it ought not define the Jesuit mission and must not overshadow, what he sees as, the more fundamental task of serving faith. For him, GC 32's turn toward justice is problematic for several reasons. First, it "too narrowly focused on human justice" and fails to take account of evangelization in its full sense.[43] Second, it risks displacing traditional ministries that may not have a clear social focus, such as teaching math and pastoral work.[44] Finally, and more profoundly, the concern for the promotion of justice may entail a "confusion" of the Jesuit priestly identity.[45]

These same concerns have been expressed by Vatican officials specifically in relation to the Jesuits. For example, in his 1982 address to Jesuit provincials, John Paul II critiqued the Jesuit turn to justice by stressing that the role of priests is different from that of the laity. Priests are not social workers, he insisted. The primary function of the priest and their ministries is not the promotion of justice but spirituality and the care of souls.[46] The new evangelization model of mission, thus raises concerns about the appropriateness for JRS and other Catholic organizations, particularly those of priests and religious, to be directly involved in the promotion of justice.

---

[41] Avery Dulles, "Faith, Justice, and the Jesuit Mission," in *Assembly 1989: Jesuit Ministry in Higher Education* (Washington, DC: Jesuit Conference, 1990), 19–25; David Hollenbach, "Faith, Justice, and the Jesuit Mission: A Response to Avery Dulles," in *Assembly 1989: Jesuit Ministry in Higher Education* (Washington, DC: Jesuit Conference, 1990), 26–29.

[42] Martin R. Tripole, *Faith Beyond Justice: Widening the Perspective* (Missouri: Institute of Jesuit Sources, 1994).

[43] Dulles, "Faith, Justice, and the Jesuit Mission," 31–32.

[44] Dulles, "Faith, Justice, and the Jesuit Mission," 25.

[45] Dulles, "Faith, Justice, and the Jesuit Mission," 76.

[46] See John Paul II, "Allocution to the Jesuit Provincials" (Vatican City: Libreria Editrice Vaticana, 1982). Here he drew from his address to an ordination ceremony, John Paul II, "Who Is the Priest? Remarks of Pope John Paul II During Ordination Ceremonies in Rio de Janeiro," *Origins* 10, no. 9 (July 31, 1980).

GOING FORTH TO THE MARGINS:
EXPANDING THE LEGACY OF *POPULORUM PROGRESSIO*
The question of how church organizations should relate to the world has taken on new dimensions with the teachings of Pope Francis. With *Evangelii Gaudium* and *Laudato Si'*, he both reclaims and expands upon the integral model of *Populorum Progressio* and *Evangelii Nuntiandi*. In some ways, this is surprising. As a Jesuit provincial and participant at the 32nd General Congregation, Jorge Mario Bergoglio expressed reservations with the justice language employed by "Decree Four" and was cautious of Jesuits who were too involved in social and political transformation.[47] He also witnessed firsthand the strengths and weaknesses of this integral model as it took shape in Latin America. Perhaps because of this experience, Francis constructs a vision of mission that seeks to navigate between two extremes.

On the one hand, like his immediate predecessors, he cautions against a narrow view that reduces mission to social transformation, a tendency that has been described as horizontalism. Frequently, for example, Francis warns against seeing the church only as another NGO. Shortly before the release of *Evangelii Gaudium*, for example, the pope stated that "the Church is not a shop, she is not a humanitarian agency, the Church is not an NGO. The Church is sent to bring Christ and his Gospel to all."[48] This is something that all church social justice organizations should take seriously.

On the other hand, like Paul VI and the 1971 Synod, Francis' model strongly warns against reducing mission only to its spiritual dimensions, what might be described as verticalism. Departing from the texts of the 2012 Synod, *Evangelii Gaudium* squarely situates the justice work of Christian social movements in the church's mission. Both as individuals and as communities, he insists, Christians are "called to be… instrument[s] of God for the liberation and promotion of the poor, and for enabling them to be fully a part of society" (no. 187). The Christian mission, he writes, must include awareness and action to "resolve the structural causes of poverty" (no. 202). Furthermore, all Christians, even those in "ecclesial circles," have an obligation to work for justice. Later, he seems to address the distinction of planes model directly. "While it is quite true," he admits, "that the essential vocation and mission of the lay faithful is to strive that earthly realities and all human activity may be transformed by the Gospel, none of us

---

[47] Jimmy Burns, *Francis, Pope of Good Promise* (New York: St. Martin's Press, 2015), 133–135.
[48] Pope Francis, "General Audience [Rome, October 23, 2013]," w2.vatican.va/content/francesco/en/audiences/2013/documents/papa-francesco_20131023_udienza-generale.html. See also Pope Francis, *Evangelii Gaudium*, no. 80.

can think we are exempt from concern for the poor and for social justice" (no. 201).

In *Laudato Si'*, Francis widens the integral model of mission to include concern for all creation with what he describes as an "integral ecology." Here, he calls upon the church to take action in the protection of creation and to inspire its members to take on "an ecological conversion" (no. 217). Later, in his 2015 address to Popular Movements in Bolivia, Francis is very clear in his call for people to organize themselves into communities for "change, real change, structural change."[49]

At the heart of Francis' prophetic model is a vision of the church that "goes forth," an apostolic community actively engaged in the world, moving out of its comfort zones and traditional ways of functioning and to the peripheries with the aim of reinstating all those who have been marginalized, socially, economically, physically, and spiritually.[50] It is a vibrant community that witnesses to God's mercy by addressing both the symptoms and root causes of human suffering.

Conclusion: Reclaiming the Legacy for Today

With *Populorum Progressio*, a new model of mission begins to take root in the church. Paul VI's integral vision of the human development necessitates a corresponding integral model of mission. In other words, if the human person is multidimensional then the proclamation of God's salvation must also be multidimensional. If people and societies are interdependent then the church's engagement in the world must go beyond borders. According to this model, which was developed further with liberation theology, *Justitia in Mundo*, and *Evangelii Nuntiandi*, the church's mission includes collective action for social transformation. This integrated framework, which has been reclaimed and developed by Francis, situates well the work of JRS and other Catholic organizations for justice.

Ultimately, what difference does it make for JRS or any other Catholic organization to link the work for social justice with the church's mission? To affirm that Catholic social justice organizations participate in the church's mission is not to claim that everything they do is perfect or that the justice positions they take are infallible. Nor is it to say that all Christians must adopt the same perspectives. On the contrary, to assert that these collectives partake in the church's mission ought to challenge the church and these organizations in several ways. First, it is necessary to affirm the ecclesial identity of such innovative

---

[49] Pope Francis, "Address of the Holy Father," World Meeting of Popular Movements, Santa Cruz, Bolivia (July 9, 2015), www.radiovaticana.va.
[50] Pope Francis, "Homily of His Holiness Pope Francis," February 15, 2015, en.radiovaticana.va/news/2015/07/10/pope_francis_speech_at_world_meeting_of_popular_movements/1157291.

apostolic agents and the role they play on behalf of the Christian community. This affirmation can bolster the moral, logistical, and even financial support that these movements receive. This should challenge Catholic organizations to reconsider how they relate to church leadership structures and other organizations with shared identities.

Second, clearly recognizing that Catholic organizations participate in the mission of the church can help to draw attention to social demands of Christian discipleship. Imagine, for instance, if JRS staff were given more spaces to share their stories in local parishes or Catholic schools in the United States. This should raise questions for parishes, schools, and other Catholic communities as to whether or not their evangelization efforts respond to the needs of all people and the whole person.

Finally, the affirmation of the ecclesial identity of Catholic social justice organizations illuminates issues and questions that ought to aid them in better pursuing their mission: including the challenge of balancing the horizontal and vertical demands of evangelization and the task of addressing questions about organizational identity and ethics. This is particularly tricky for organizations, like JRS, who serve and employ non-Catholic staff. A more robust integral missiology can help these organizations better avoid the dangers of either focusing too much on their social dimension or focusing too much on their spiritual dimension.

Given the complex challenges facing the human family today, Catholic organizations, like JRS, need better missiological models to witness to the Gospel in the world. Here, *Populorum Progressio*'s integral vision of mission, and its renewed attention in the teachings of Pope Francis, can be constructive in offering a framework that can enable the church to respond to the needs of all those who desire the good news of the Gospel. Ⓜ

Journal of Moral Theology, Vol. 6, No. 1 (2017): 57-79

The Enduring Significance of *Populorum Progressio* for the Church in Africa

Stan Chu Ilo

F LYING BACK TO ROME after his five day "pilgrimage of peace" as an "apostle of hope" to Africa in November 2015, Pope Francis, in answer to a question on the most memorable part of his trip, said, "For me, Africa was a surprise. God always surprises us, but Africa surprises us too. I remember many moments, but above all, I remember the crowds…They felt visited, they are incredibly welcoming and I saw this in all three nations." Pope Francis spoke of Africa as a continent of hope and Bangui, the capital of Central African Republic, as the "spiritual capital of the world." Francis had a clear message to all: "Africa is a martyr of exploitation," "Africa is a victim of other powers." For Pope Francis, Africa is "perhaps the world's richest continent," "Africa is a land of hope."[1]

With the election of Pope Francis in 2013, a new impetus has been given in Catholicism to some of the main themes of Catholic social teaching—poverty, human dignity and rights, family life, the rights of minorities, death penalty, reconciliation, international development, solidarity, income inequality, migration, justice and peace, aid and outreach to the poor, climate change, population, and a critique of neoliberal capitalism. Pope Francis has been a strong advocate for the Global South, especially in his message on how unequal power structures in the world and unequal economic relations work against the will of God for the world.[2] This essay attempts to show how African Catholicism has been in the forefront for the realization of God's dream in Africa since the publication of *Populorum Progressio*. The social mission of the Church in Africa is one of the most important and significant aspects of African Catholicism. I wish to show in this essay how this social mission emerged, the context in which it is flourishing in Africa, and the challenges which it faces.

---

[1] "In-Flight Press Conference of His Holiness Pope Francis from the Central African Republic to Rome," w2.vatican.va/content/francesco/en/speeches/2015/november/documents/papa-francesco_20151130_repubblica-centrafricana-conferenza-stampa.html.

[2] See Pope Francis, "Address at the United Nations Office in Nairobi, 26 November, 2015," in *Messages of Pope Francis During His Apostolic Journey to Africa, 25-30 November, 2015* (Kenya: Paulines Publications Africa, 2015), 19-25.

This essay is divided into two parts. In the first part, I explore the enduring significance of *Populorum Progressio* in Africa by identifying some key themes in this important encyclical with regard to the African social context. I analyze the key theological and pastoral developments in the Church's social mission in Africa as a result of *Populorum Progressio*. In the second part, I explore five factors limiting genuine development. These are the needs to overcome a linear notion of history, to listen to the poor, to change problematic notions of development, to accurately understand the causes of poverty, and to include women.

THE ENDURING SIGNIFICANCE OF *POPULORUM PROGRESSIO*

According to Peter Hebblethwaite, Pope Paul VI "did his reputation a world of good with *Populorum Progressio*."[3] The reputation of Pope Paul VI soared in Africa with this encyclical because he gave a broader foundation to the teaching of Vatican II, especially *Gaudium et Spes*, through the emphasis on the social mission of the Church, integral development, and, more particularly, the mission to the poor in newly independent countries in the Global South. In this regard, Donal Dorr writes, "what *Populorum Progressio* gives is a framework or anticipation of the 'shape' of genuine human development. In technical terms what it offers is a 'heuristic' notion of development."[4] Dorr adds that the heuristic concept of development undertakes socio-ethical analysis of development beyond merely technical, theoretical and economic accounts.[5] In charting this new path, Paul VI began a process of widening the understanding of poverty beyond simply "growing out" of poverty, "catching up" with the West, and "ensuring the proper distribution of existing wealth and resources."[6] In *Populorum Progressio*, Paul VI gave a new synthesis and update of Catholic social teaching, while offering theological justifications for the Church's ethical principles on the development of peoples, social justice, Christian humanism and a new hermeneutics for reading the movement of history.

The Church at Vatican II did not succeed in pushing forward a specific document on global poverty, inequality, and economic, social, and political turmoil afflicting emerging nations in the Global South. In addition, Vatican II did not offer a strong framework for doing social analysis which could help the Church in Africa to diagnose the

---

[3] Peter Hebblethwaite, *Paul VI: The First Modern Pope* (New York: Paulist Press, 1993), 483.
[4] Donal Dorr, *Option for the Poor: A Hundred Years of Vatican Social Teaching*, *Revised Edition* (New York: Orbis Books, 1992), 181.
[5] Dorr, *Option for the Poor*, 182-183.
[6] Dorr, *Option for the Poor*, 179.

African predicament through the lens of Catholic social teaching. Instead, Paul VI in *Populorum Progressio* redefined the trajectory of the discussion within the Church and in global politics on the grinding poverty afflicting humanity and the inequality and human suffering to which many people were subjected, especially outside the West. He thus provided a key to a social analytical vector for understanding global poverty through the compass of a new Catholic understanding of development and the questions of human rights, economic and political systems, and social justice. All the questions raised in *Populorum Progressio* were central to the conversations going on in Africa in the 1960s and beyond about the directions of history in newly independent nations of Africa. Thus, Pope Paul set the direction of discourse on Catholic social teaching in Africa in the post-Vatican II Church in many ways.

Africa Needs Her Own Narrative of Faith and Social Mission
    Pope Paul VI was concerned that Africa must develop her own narrative of faith and social mission. Unlike Pope Pius XII, who was more concerned that Africa should acknowledge and embrace Europe's contribution to Africa's progress and warned African bishops in the 1950s against "blind nationalism" which could lead Africa into "chaos and slavery," Paul VI was a strong advocate for Africa's own unique narratives of faith, life, and society.[7] He became the first modern Pontiff to visit Africa where he experienced firsthand, as he did in India, some of the pressing social questions facing newly independent countries in Africa and Asia. During this visit, Paul VI gave the now famous battle cry to Africa that the time was ripe for a truly African Church.[8] In his famous speech of 1969 in Kampala, he underlined the need for African solutions to African problems—social, political, economic, theological, and cultural. However, he had already visited Africa in 1962 as Cardinal Montini, and, in 1964 as pope, he canonized the Ugandan martyrs at St. Peter's Basilica. Thus, he made the history and contribution of African Christianity central to ongoing conversations at Vatican II and the history and contributions of non-Western churches to the future direction of world affairs and world Christianity.
    His homily at the canonization was remarkable in many ways. He not only highlighted the spiritual treasures of Africa, but he also pointed to Africa's central place in salvation history and in the history of humanity. Furthermore, while emphasizing that human suffering and persecution still afflicted Africa, especially in the decolonization

---

[7] Robert Calderisi, *Earthly Mission: The Catholic Church and World Development* (Connecticut: Yale University Press, 2013), 108.
[8] Paul VI, "Address to the Symposium of Episcopal Conferences of Africa and Madagascar, Kampala," *Acta Apostolicae Sedis* 61 (1969): 575.

process, he made a very painful assertion about Africa's need to make a transition from her primitive civilization which highlighted the negative interpretation of Africa as backward and in need of integration into civilization (i.e., Western and Christian) in order to overcome the incubus of her benighted past.[9] This is a point which is still prevalent in Western humanitarianism to Africa, that is, the idea of Africa as trapped, backward, and needy.

Africae Terrarum *and Pope Paul VI's Vision for the Church's Social Mission in Africa*

The most developed and comprehensive form of Paul VI's vision for African development where he advances key themes and theological principles in *Populorum Progressio* with a specific reference to the African social context is the papal message, *Land of Africa* (*Africae Terrarum*).[10] This document was published less than six months after the publication of *Populorum Progressio* on 29 October, 1967. Because of its importance in understanding the continuing significance of *Populorum Progressio* in Africa and the future of the Church's social mission in Africa, it is important to highlight four of the key themes offered in this document.

The first is in article 6 where Paul VI called for a sober realism about the fundamental challenges facing post-independence Africa beyond the euphoria of independence and the innocent ideals which were captured in the hope of a cultural renaissance. This was characterized by a triumphalism that romanticized a progressive future of prosperity which was opening to Africa following the end of colonial rule. This optimism was captured in the now famous slogan by the African nationalist and first President of Ghana, Kwame Nkrumah, who said, "Seek ye first the political kingdom (i.e. independence) and every other thing shall be added unto thee." Paul VI was a sobering voice in this regard in calling the attention of Africa to the fact that hope is not achievement and that development was more than a word. Indeed, at the time of the publication of *Populorum Progressio*, post-independ-

---

[9] See 30Days, "Paul VI and the Memory of the African Marytrs," www.30giorni.it/articoli_id_1199_l3.htm: "These African martyrs open a new epoch....The tragedy which devoured them is so unheard of and expressive as to offer representative elements sufficient for the moral formation of a new people, for the foundation of a new spiritual tradition, to symbolize and to *promote the passage from a primitive civilization*, [emphasis added] not lacking in magnificent human values, but infected and weak and almost a slave of itself, to a civilization open to the superior expressions of the spirit and to superior forms of social life."

[10] This message was released in Latin. I am using the translation in French, but the numbering both in the French and Latin versions are the same. See "Message a l'Afrique, de 1967: *Africae Terrarum*, Adresse à la Hiérarchie de L'Eglise Catholique d'Afrique et Tous les Peuple de ce Continent," in Tharcisse T. Tshibangu, *Le Concile Vatican II et L'Eglise Africaine* (Paris: Epiphanie-Karthala, 2012), 103-122.

ence Africa was actually living in a delicate situation requiring national dialogue, collaboration, solidarity, and planning. These steps were considered more decisive in helping African nations consolidate what they had achieved with the end of colonialism rather than mere optimism and euphoria of a renascent Africa.

The second point which Paul VI makes is about contextualization of development practices and local ownership of development. In nos. 7-15 of *Africae Terrarum*, he returns to a theme which he already emphasized in *Populorum Progressio*, nos. 40-41 and 64 on respect for indigenous knowledge, authentic religious, cultural and economic values and patterns. This is grounded on the "heuristic notion" of development, that is, the notion that integral development goes beyond economic systems and orthodoxies imposed by one culture over another. Development is not a gift which one culture gives to another. Thus, development should not be considered simply as the translation of socio-theoretical constructs and models of social progress developed in one milieu and transferred to another with determinate consequences or results. In *Populorum Progressio*, no. 40, Paul VI noted that "rich or poor, each country possesses a civilization handed down by their ancestors: institutions called for by life in this world, and higher manifestations of the life of the spirit, manifestations of an artistic, intellectual and religious character. When the latter possess true human values, it would be a grave error to sacrifice them to the former." He was emphatic in *Populorum Progressio*, no. 64 on the need to respect in countries outside the non-Western civilization "their own proper genius, the means for their social and human progress."

This is a call which is gaining greater currency today with the failure of many development and aid initiatives in Africa. At the UN Third High Level Forum on Aid Effectiveness in Accra, Ghana in 2008, the international community agreed that of the five factors in effective development and aid initiatives—ownership, alignment, harmonization, managing results, and mutual accountability—local ownership of development policies and practices (through local knowledge, local agenda, etc.) is the most critical and decisive step. However, this was a point which Paul VI was so prescient in highlighting more than 30 years before the Paris Declaration (2005) where the idea of failed development practices and exogenous economic programs in the Global South was first discussed as a prelude to the midterm evaluation of the Millennium Development Goals in 2006.

Third, Paul VI did not just enunciate these principles, he also gave the rationale in *Africae Terrarum* for why the Church and international organizations must respect local knowledge and contextualization of development principles and praxis. The foundation for the principles and praxis of development, according to him, is a theological foundation which in Africa is already grounded in an African spirituality, family life, communitarian spirit, and a moral tradition of abundant life as human and cosmic flourishing (*Africae Terrarum*, nos. 12-14). According to Pope Paul, the development of technical and scientific skills in Africa's march towards modernity should not sacrifice Africa's moral tradition or values which make for the good of order but should be transmitted and incarnated through these essential values (*Africae Terrarum*, no. 12). Rather, development in Africa must be housed in local processes and mediated through local knowledge.

Fourth is the connection between poverty and conflict and the need to place human and cultural development in nations above technical solutions. According to Paul VI, the only path for avoiding wars and conflict in nations and between nations in Africa is through a just society where everyone has equal access to the common good. Despite the challenges and conflicts which afflicted Africa in 1967, with the Nigerian-Biafran War and the Congo conflicts among others, Paul VI believed there were signs of hope in Africa. However, he warned that the kind of violent conflicts afflicting African countries caused by ethnocentric sentiments could lead to genocide if not contained. This was a prophetic statement through which one could read such genocidal conflicts and crimes against humanity in Nigeria (1967-1970), Darfur, Northern Uganda, Rwanda, the Democratic Republic of Congo, and the Central African Republic among others.[11] Most importantly, the recipe for peace in Africa and for the world for Paul VI is "the participation of all the citizens in the construction of a new society that would encourage public programs at the governmental level and private initiatives of associations" (*Africae Terrarum*, no. 16).

Paul VI sees the causes and cure of poverty and suffering revolving around the question of justice in the world. According to Bernard Brady, a significant aspect of *Populorum Progressio* is Paul VI's insistence that the condition for a global order lies in justice in the world and peace achieved through the integral development of every part of the world. This, for Paul VI, requires "deep respect for and responsibility to the marginalized and powerless throughout the world."[12] Paul VI proposes that poverty and injustice rather than ideological differences will define the nature and complexion of future global conflict.

Paul VI's social encyclical was one of the earliest cries to the world to embrace an ethics of compassion, solidarity, charity and justice, especially for those on the margins, in order to avoid wars. This was why he made that famous statement that the name of development is peace

---

[11] See Karen E. Smith, "The UK and 'Genocide' in Biafra," in *Journal of Genocide Research* 16, no. 2-3 (2014): 247-262. See also Paul VI, "Lettre Du Pape Paul VI Signee Par Le Cardinal A. Cicognani, Secretaire D'Etat, A S.E. Yakubu Gowon, Chef Du Governement Miliataire Federal de Lagos, Julliet, 1967," w2.vatican.va/content/paul-vi/fr/letters/1967/documents/hf_p-vi_let_19670701_cap-governo-nigeria.html.
[12] Bernard V. Brady, *Essential Catholic Social Thought* (Maryknoll, NY: Orbis Books, 2008), 134.

because "to wage war on misery and to struggle against injustice is to promote, along with improved conditions, the human and spiritual progress of all men and therefore the common good of humanity" (*Populorum Progressio*, no. 76). His was a clear-sighted prophetic message that the history of the world cannot evolve towards human and cosmic flourishing while a majority of the people of the earth are abandoned in the lower rungs of economic and social progress. As Hebblethwaite rightly noted, Paul VI was prophetic in predicting that future global conflict will not be between the East and the West, but rather between the North and South.[13]

Paul VI's proposals for African development could be summarized in nos. 17-19 to include: (i) a social and economic program which should cut across ethnocentric particularism but must include civic education for promoting the common good; (ii) a rejection of racism and all practices and programs at the international or local levels which insult the dignity of the human person while being faithful to the teachings of Vatican II and *Populorum Progressio*; (iii) the promotion of universal solidarity and global action to bring about a better world through justice and peace. In this regard, the Church he proposes must play an essential part in defending human rights and social justice while emphasizing the just distribution of national wealth; (iv) the necessity of international aid to Africa because, as he noted, Africa was in dire straits and needed solidarity to help kick start her development. However, such aid must not blind Africa to confronting what Paul VI sees (no. 20) as two fundamental challenges facing her in order to achieve integral development, namely the education of her populace and improving her agricultural production by adopting modern methods of farming. These are two essential messages which he already addressed in *Populorum Progressio* (nos. 65, 46, 54, 62). In showing solidarity to Africa through aid, Paul VI goes back again to the message of *Populorum Progressio* that aid and development are not ends in themselves but means to capacity-building and should not lead to dependency or a new form of colonialism (no. 52).

These four principles are still valid today in understanding why, after more than 50 years of different approaches to development and aid in Africa, no significant progress has been made in transforming the lives of Africans. When one explores the evolution of Catholic social ethics with regard to development in Africa, from the time of the publication of *Populorum Progressio* to the Second African Synod (2009), one can see why the message of Paul VI is still valid today in the development of the theological principles which inform the social mission of the Church in Africa.

---

[13] Hebblethwaite, *Paul VI*, 483.

The Impact of Populorum Progressio *on the Catholic Social Mission in Africa*

Populorum Progressio had decisive and far reaching effects in the evolution of the Church's social ministry in general and the social mission in Africa in particular. The pope rejected unequivocally many of the basic precepts of capitalism, including the unrestricted private ownership of means of production, the uncontrolled desire for profit to the detriment of the poor, and the rough edges of free trade. He also drew attention to the unequal development of people in the developing countries, the scourge of poverty, and imperialism which continued to hold many peoples and nations in chains.[14]

The encyclical gave a new impetus to the work of the newly constituted Pontifical Commission for Justice and Peace (created in January 1967 by Pope Paul VI as an ecclesial initiative and structure authorized by Vatican II). In addition, this commission fostered a global Catholic movement which became like a sentinel leading to a more active involvement of the Catholic Church in worldwide causes for justice and peace. It helped to deepen global Catholic conversation on the role of the Church in the world and to establish justice and peace commissions in parishes, dioceses, and episcopal conference offices, as well as in many Vatican congregations, councils, and committees.[15]

In Africa, this led to the creation of diocesan and national offices for justice and peace and a more coordinated organization of church charities. However, the Church moved faster in Latin America than in Africa in translating the message of Paul VI into local idioms with its strong emphasis on the option for the poor at the 1968 Medellín conference and the emergence of liberation theology as a distinctive social analysis and praxis of transformation informed by the Christian Gospel. In Africa, the impact of *Populorum Progressio* was much slower. The African bishops in 1981 admitted that they did not do enough to advance and contextualize the message of *Populorum Progressio* within the broader picture of the social mission of the Church.[16] However, between the First and Second African Synods (1994-2009), there were significant developments in Africa in deepening the understanding of the theology and praxis of the Church's social mission.

Many factors led to this new impetus. There was the theological development in African Catholicism on Catholic social teaching and social analysis by theologians like Adrian Hastings, Engelvert Mveng, Jean-Mac Ela, Elochukwu Uzukwu, Benezet Bujo, Laurenti Magesa,

---

[14] See David J. O'Brien and Thomas A. Shannon, *Catholic Social Thought: A Documentary Heritage* (New York: Orbis Books, 1992), 238–239.

[15] For a more detailed discussion of the worldwide Catholic movement for justice and peace, see Joseph Gremillion, *The Gospel of Peace and Justice: Catholic Social Teaching Since Pope John* (New York: Orbis Books, 1976), 188–190.

[16] Calderisi, *Earthly Mission*, 60.

and Pete Henriot. Added to this was the introduction of studies of Catholic social teaching in many African seminaries, colleges and universities led by religious orders like the Jesuits in Eastern, Southern and Central Africa, Comboni and Maryknoll Fathers in East Africa, the White Fathers in West Africa, and the Loretto sisters in Southern Africa. Particularly, these predominantly foreign congregations and missions began to introduce in their congregations, especially after the 1974 synod on evangelization, a reflective practice to their charitable work. Also significant in this regard was the pastoral, biblical, and social formation that was taking place in the flourishing small Christian communities in African parishes and local communities. However, not all Africans warmed up to missionaries leading the social mission in Africa. Between 1971 and 1974 there was a strong movement for a self-governing, self-reliant, and self-reproducing African Church.

This movement led to the 1974 All African Conference of Churches' (AACC) Lusaka declaration for a moratorium on missionaries and money being sent to Africa. This declaration supported by some Catholic clerics read in part:

> To enable the African Church to achieve the power of becoming a true instrument of liberating and reconciling the African people, as well as finding solutions to economic and social dependency, our option as a matter of policy has to be a moratorium on external assistance in money and personnel. We recommend this option as the only potent means of becoming truly and authentically ourselves while remaining a respected and responsible part of the Universal Church.[17]

The Catholic Church is not a member of the AACC, but the document submitted by the African Catholic bishops on co-responsibility to the 1974 synod spoke in part on the need for Africa to assume full responsibility for her mission, theologies, pastoral life, and social ministry.

Another important development worthy of note was the publication and dissemination of Catholic literature and magisterial documents through the *African Ecclesial Review*, the first English speaking Catholic journal in Africa which began publication in 1959 and devoted a special section to recent papal and magisterial teachings. The publication was supplemented by Paulines Publications Africa which, since its inception in 1981, has remained the greatest source for the dissemination of Catholic literature in Africa.

---

[17] Quoted in Adrian Hastings, *African Christianity: An Essay in Interpretation* (London: Geoffrey Chapman, 1976), 22.

But the most important factor was that some of the most pressing issues being discussed in Catholic social teaching were already ravaging Africa in the 1970s—wars, grinding poverty, dictatorial governments, drought, locust invasion, tension over mission and money, foreign aid, neo-colonial factors, and the impact of the West-East ideological battles in Africa. These factors created multiple interventionist measures in Africa both by international organizations as well as Catholic charities. There was an urgent need to articulate how to proceed with aid initiatives in Africa and development discourse in African Catholic theology. This required some specific African approaches for social analysis informed by Catholic social teaching against the backdrop of the growing reliance of emerging African voices on liberation theology and Black liberationist discourse which were becoming suspect, especially in Roman circles.

Another area of strong participation by the Catholic Church inspired by *Populorum Progressio* was in building civil society and protecting human rights. This is still a very complex area in Catholic social teaching because the Church and her officials are supposed to be neutral and non-partisan. There are many questions which emerge in the light of recent history in Africa. Why should the Church be nonpartisan in the face of misrule, corruption, inexcusable human suffering, and the collapse of law and order in some parts of Africa? Why should the Church be neutral in Africa in the face of genocide and a culture of waste or glaring cases of injustice perpetrated against minorities because of ethnicity, gender, religion, and social class?

Many Catholic clerics abandoned neutrality of any kind and soon became champions of human rights and voices for the poor and the marginalized. While some of them did not leave behind enormous writings, the witness of their lives gave voice to the principles of Catholic social teaching. The Catholic Archbishop Christophe Munzihirwa of Bukavu (DRC), who was one of the most vocal critics of the misrule of Mobutu Sese Seko, was assassinated by Rwandan troops in Eastern Zaire and his corpse left on the streets for many days. Archbishop Luwum of Uganda was murdered on the orders of the dictator Idi Amin in 1977 because of his open condemnation of the malfeasance of the so-called "butcher of Uganda." In the same year, Catholic Cardinal Émile Biayenda was murdered in the political strife in the two Congos; he was a defender of human rights and a culture of good governance and justice for the ordinary people in the 1970s. In West Africa, the heroism of Cardinals Bernard Yago of Abidjan, Paul Zoungrana of Ouagadogou, and Olubunmi Okojie of Lagos are still commonly referred to as some of the earliest indications in African

Catholicism of a prophetic witness to the social Gospel.[18] Many Catholic clerics headed or served in constitutional conferences and truth and reconciliation commissions which ushered in constitutional democracies in DRC, Sierra Leone, Liberia, Nigeria, Benin, and Côte d'Ivoire. These are the earliest indications out of many of how Catholic involvement in Africa's democratic process was born. Absent from all these, however, were the voices of women, which is a major challenge facing the Church in her social mission in Africa, especially in the areas of civic culture, governance, and leadership.

By the time of the Second African Synod (2009), the Catholic Church in Africa was regarded as the biggest NGO in Africa in terms of her social mission. Compared to other religious organizations and private agencies working in the healthcare industry in Africa for example, the Catholic Church had the largest number of private hospitals and clinics providing medical care, free medical treatment for HIV/AIDS patients in some cases, and services for pregnant women and people suffering from malaria and other tropical diseases. This happened even in those African countries where the Catholic Church was not a majority. In Ghana for instance, Catholics made up about 30% of the population, but the Catholic Church had more hospitals than any other private agency in the country.

The impact of the Catholic Church is also visible in many other social sectors in Africa. In Uganda for example, the Catholic Church is the second largest provider of vocational, technical, teacher, and business training (22% of student numbers compared to the government's 42%). The Catholic Church provides 28% of the country's hospital beds.[19] In Africa, the Church works in 16,178 health centers, including 1,074 hospitals, 5,373 out-patient clinics, 186 leper colonies, 753 homes for the elderly and physically and mentally less able brothers and sisters, 979 orphanages, 1,997 kindergartens, 1,590 marriage counseling centers, 2,947 social re-education centers and 1,279 other various centers. There are 12,496 nursery schools with 1,266,444 registered children; 33,263 primary schools with 14,061,000 pupils and 9,838 high schools with 3,738,238 students. Some 54,362 students are enrolled in higher institutes, of which 11,011 are pursuing ecclesiastical studies. There are 53 national chapters of Caritas, 34 national commissions of justice and peace, and 12 institutes and centers promoting the social doctrine of the Church, the most notable of which are the African Forum for Catholic Social Teaching (AFCAST) in Harare, Zimbabwe, the Center for the Study of Catholic Social Teaching, at the Catholic University of Eastern Africa in Kenya, the Jesuit Center

---

[18] See Philip Jenkins, *The Next Christendom: The Coming of Global Christianity, Third Edition* (Oxford: Oxford University Press, 2011), 182-184.
[19] Calderisi, *Earthly Mission*, 112.

for Social Justice in Lusaka, Zambia, the Catholic Institute for Development Justice and Peace, in Enugu, Nigeria, the Gaba Institute in Eldoret, Kenya, the Centre de Recherche et Du Action de La Paix (CERAP) in Abidjan, Côte d'Ivoire, and the Songhai Farms in Porto-Novo, Benin, to mention but a few.

CHALLENGES TO DEVELOPMENT

While *Populorum Progressio* ushered in advances in Catholic social teaching and spurred the social mission of the Church in Africa, there are still challenges hindering the kind of development called for by Paul VI. In what follows, I highlight five needs for true development in Africa: to overcome a linear notion of history, to listen to the poor, to change problematic notions of development, to accurately understand the causes of poverty, and to include women.

The Need to Overcome a Linear Notion of History

Writing on the significance of *Populorum Progressio* in the evolution of Catholic social teaching, Peter Henriot argues that *Populorum Progressio* offers the most complete statement on integral development in Catholic social teaching.[20] While there has been evolution in the "principles of reflection, norms of judgment and directives for action" on integral development in such documents as *Caritas in Veritate*, *Evangelium Gaudium*, *Laudate Si'*, *Sollicitudo Rei Socialis*, and *Laborem Exercens*, the main anthropological, theological, and cultural framework has remained the same.[21] This framework created a challenge to Africa.

Paul VI defines development in many parts of *Populorum Progressio*, the most significant being that "Development cannot be limited to mere economic growth. In order to be authentic, it must be complete: integral, that is, it has to promote the good of every man and the whole man" (no. 43). He also teaches that development is the new name for peace (no. 76), and that "to speak of development, is in effect to show as much concern for social progress as for economic growth" and that "there can be no progress towards the complete development of man without the simultaneous development of all humanity in the spirit of solidarity" (no. 43). The aim of all development according to Paul VI is "complete humanism" which is not closed in on itself but open to the Absolute. According to Benedict XVI, this insight on development was perhaps the most important contribution of Paul VI in *Populorum Progressio*. According to Pope Benedict in *Caritas in Veritate*,

---

[20] Peter J. Henriot, "Who Cares About Africa? Development Guidelines from the Church's Social Teaching," in *Catholic Social Thought and the New World Order*, ed. Oliver F. Williams and John W. Houck (Indiana: University of Notre Dame Press, 1993), 209.

[21] Henriot, "Who Cares About Africa?" 209-210.

The truth of development consists in its completeness: if it does not involve the whole man and every man, it is not true development. This is the central message of *Populorum Progressio*, valid for today and for all time. Integral human development on the natural plane, as a response to a vocation from God the Creator, demands self-fulfillment in a "transcendent humanism which gives him greatest possible perfection: this is the highest goal of personal development." The Christian vocation to this development therefore applies to both the natural plane and the supernatural plane; which is why, "when God is eclipsed our ability to recognize the natural order, purpose and the good begins to wane." (no. 15)

Paul VI was ahead of his times in proposing a holistic understanding of development which has been adopted by the UN, national governments, and other international organizations since the turn of the millennium. Indeed, the Millennium Development Goals (MDGs) and the Sustainable Development Goals (SDGs) of the UN all show an understanding of development beyond economics. There are many aspects of human and cosmic life which do not show up on the GDP or per capital income. This is the realization that led to the formation of the World Faiths Development Dialogue by the World Bank in 1998 and the Faith in Development partnership between the World Bank and the churches of Africa in 2000.

Former World Bank President James D. Wolfensohn writes that he came to realize over the course of his tenure "how far religious ideas and attitudes" are linked to development and imbue every facet of society with "social trust and cohesion." He argues further that, "religion has an effect on many peoples' attitudes to everything including such matters as savings, investment and a host of economic decisions. It influences areas we had come to see as vital for successful development, like schooling, gender equality, and approaches to healthcare. In short, religion could be an important driver of change, even as it could be a brake to progress."[22] Along the same line of argument, the World Social Forum's document, "Faith and the Global Agenda: Values for the Post-Crisis Economy," highlights the role of religion in helping humanity to rethink the development of the moral framework and the regulatory mechanism that underpin the economy, politics, and global inter-connectedness.[23] The deeply religious worldview of Africa is a veritable framework which must be harvested in the social

---

[22] James D. Wolfensohn, "Foreword," in *Religion and Development: Ways of Transforming the World*, ed. Gerrie ter Haar (London: Hurst and Company, 2011), xvii.
[23] Quoted in Garrie Ter Haar, "Religion and Development: Introducing a Debate," in *Religion and Development*, 9.

ministry of the Church in Africa. This is because it sees human and cosmic flourishing as intimately connected in a bond of life which is not often reflected in the Western linear, secular, and progressive notion of history or modernity.

While development in *Populorum Progressio* shares some common values with the African notion of abundant life in placing the human person and communities as the goal of all development, an African understanding of community is theandrocosmic (God-humans-cosmos) rather than anthropocentric. Community is understood in African social ethics as the whole of the visible and non-visible universe that includes water, hills, trees, animals, human beings, neighbors, the living and the living-dead, the not-yet-born, God, and spirits. This holistic notion of community is very eco-spiritual because abundant life is understood as the condition which exists when the whole of creation is flourishing because they have fullness of life. This goes beyond the restricted anthropocentric and transcendental notions of integral development in *Populorum Progressio*.

Populorum Progressio and African theologies of development share a strong emphasis on integral development as grounded in a spiritual and cosmic vision of life beyond the false economic messianism of development experts and development theories. However, the African religio-cultural worldview removes itself from the determinism of a linear history built on an economic orthodoxy. African theologies of development-as-abundant life for human and cosmic flourishing are holistic. They move toward a more critical and broader reading of history and development by examining the root causes of poverty and the African predicament. They seek spiritual, cultural, historical, and economic causative factors for the African condition and propose solutions which will reverse the effects of these factors. They are harvesting alternative pathways to the future through narratives of hope in the counter-development subalterns that are new stories of belonging, healing, and restoration in local communities away from the lime light of celebrities and humanitarian tourists. The whole theological structure on which Paul VI builds his teaching on development is based on a linear sense of history, Western worldview, binaries and dualisms—heaven/earth, secular/profane, church/state, poverty/wealth, present/future—in philosophy, theology, anthropology, eschatology, and cosmology.[24] As the Indian economist Deepak Lal rightly noted with regard to the genealogy of social theories, the progressive notion of history, development, and the perfectibility of the human person are

---

[24] See for instance Allan Figueroa Deck, "Commentary on *Populorum Progressio* (On the Development of Peoples)," in *Modern Catholic Social Teaching: Commentaries and Interpretations*, ed. Kenneth R. Himes, et al. (Washington, DC: Georgetown University Press, 2004), 302.

"actually part of a culture-specific, proselytizing ethic of what remains at the heart of Western Christendom."[25]

The Need to Listen to the Poor

In 2000, the UN published a significant finding on the definition of poverty within the context of its plan to develop a policy on poverty and development. The book was a field study conducted in 1999 involving over 20,000 poor women and men from 23 countries. According to Deepa Narayan, one of the authors, the formulation of any policy on poverty and development in the 21st century must be informed by those who know most about poverty, "their voices, their experiences, and their recommendations."[26] Yet, so often the voices of the poor are neglected. He writes, "There are 2.8 billion poverty experts, the poor themselves. Yet the development discourse about poverty has been dominated by the perspectives and expertise of those who are not poor – professionals, politicians and agency officials."[27]

The authors found from this research that despite very different political, social, and economic contexts, there are striking similarities in poor people's experiences. One of these common themes in poor people's experiences was one of powerlessness.[28] Complementing this research – reinforced in a study by Oxfam of one hundred transformational, locally-driven projects in different parts of the world—is the decisiveness of human agency.[29] The agency of Africa must become the means for the construction of Africa's present and future development; it must begin with recognizing the assets and gift of the people. As the World Council of Churches document *Together Towards Life* clearly stated,

> Living on the margins, however, can provide its own lessons. People on the margins have agency, and can often see what, from the centre, is out of view. People on the margins, living in vulnerable positions, often know what exclusionary forces are threatening their survival and can best discern the urgency of their struggles; people in positions of privilege have much to learn from the daily struggles of people living in marginal conditions."[30]

---

[25] Quoted in Ter Haar, "Religion and Development," 17.

[26] Deepa Narayan, "Voices of the Poor," in *Faith in Development: Partnership Between the World Bank and the Churches of Africa*, ed. Deryke Belshaw, Robert Calderisi, and Chris Sgden (Oxford: Regnum Books International, 2001), 39.

[27] Deepa Narayan, Robert Chambers, Meera K. Shah, and Patti Petesch, *Voices of the Poor Crying out for Change* (New York: Oxford University Press, 2000), 21.

[28] Narayan et al., *Voices of the Poor Crying out for Change*, 21.

[29] See Duncan Green, *From Poverty to Power: How Active Citizens and Effective States Can Change the World* (Oxford: Oxfam International, 2012).

[30] World Council of Churches, "Together Towards Life: Mission and Evangelization in Changing Landscapes," archived.oikoumene.org/en/resources/documents/wcc-

The Need to Change Problematic Notions of Development

Between 1967 when *Populorum Progressio* was published and 2013 when Pope Francis took office, one can identify five forms of mainstream development initiatives in Africa: Church social mission administered by the clergy and religious in Africa, and mainly driven by laity from the West (CSM); celebrity humanitarianism (CH); African development led by Western experts and international organizations (ADW); Religious Enchantment over Social Action (RESA); and Governmental Economic and Technical Development Agenda (GETDA). I highlight their commonalities and show the limitations of these approaches to development and social mission.

First, the common rationale for development initiatives in Africa since post-independence is the integration of Africa into the global economy. Driven by the modernization theory which seeks greater convergence in the global economy, the central argument for these approaches is that poverty in Africa and other non-Western societies is the result of a divergence in technical, political, cultural, religious, and economic life from the West. In other words, Africa needs to become like the West in adopting political and constitutional democratic principles and Western economic orthodoxies in order to bridge the yawning gap between the quality of life in Africa and the West.

The second characteristic is that these approaches have very rigid operational principles. These are often out of sync with local practices and initiatives, cultural understandings, and indigenous knowledge for creating wealth. In other words, a lot of development initiatives in Africa are defined by economic, technical, and operational principles originating outside of Africa. Even the economic theories are driven by mainstream economic orthodoxies which often do not take cognizance of Africa's own unique world of business and the high cultural contextual framework of African communal and social life. When these economic structural frameworks transplanted into Africa fail— as they do in such policies as Structural Adjustment Programs (SAPs), the Lagos and Cairo Plans of Action, African Alternative Framework to Structural Adjustment Programs, the New Partnership for African Development (NEPAD)—the clinical economists of the World Bank, IMF, Washington Consensus group of lenders, or G8 blame Africa rather than admit their structural incoherence in the African context.[31]

This rigidity in operational principles and practices is not a challenge peculiar to secular organizations. It is also a challenge to

---

commissions/mission-and-evangelism/together-towards-life-mission-and-evange-lism-in-changing-landscapes.html.
[31] See Eddy Maloka, *Africa's Development Thinking Since Independence: A Reader* (Pretoria: African Institute of South Africa, 2002).

churches working in Africa. Most of the operational principles for running church charities—Caritas, papal charities, CAFOD, Missio, Misereor, or the USCCB office of International Justice and Peace—are set outside Africa and read the African predicament through the narrow lens of poverty and suffering. These development initiatives also frame Africa more in terms of what she needs rather than what she can offer her peoples and the world. Church social mission in Africa is still predominantly run by local bishops, priests, and nuns who set the agenda, write the proposals, and implement the projects without accountability to the poor people, while sometimes neglecting the agency and voices of the poor.

The future of the social mission of the Church in Africa must be constructed outside of top-down hierarchical thinking, planning, implementation and reporting. The principles and practices for the social mission of the Church in Africa should not simply be the translation of models designed abroad. The social mission of the Church in Africa needs to be concrete, grounded in local processes, paying particular attention to local narratives and initiatives. The social mission of the Church in Africa must harvest the riches of African construction of abundant life rather than being informed by aid from abroad. The future of African development and the Church's mission in Africa does not lie in African bishops and priests begging the West, but lies in new forms of being Church which are determined by the context and agency of Africans.

This was the intention of Paul VI's speech inaugurating the Justice and Peace Commissions after the publication of *Populorum Progressio*. He wanted local parishes, dioceses, and national commissions of justice and peace to "keep the eye of the church alert, her heart open, and her hand outstretched for the work of love she is called upon to do." As Hebblethwaite noted, the whole goal of this was to give power to local churches in discerning the signs of the times in their communities.[32] The Church's mission in Africa cannot be achieved through synods and meetings, through fundraising abroad, or by foreign aid. The Church's social mission in Africa cannot be achieved through occasional "development tourists" like Western Church leaders and missionaries who spend so much money to do in Africa the work which Africans can and should do for themselves. The social mission of the Church must begin first by paying attention to the assets and initiatives of the primary drivers of grassroots transformation in Africa.

The third characteristic of these development initiatives is an emphasis on needs rather than assets. The history of Africa's contact with the outside world, especially within the last one hundred years, has been one of unequal power relations, exploitation, and failure to understand and engage Africa at a level beyond the narratives of poverty,

---

[32] See Hebblethwaite, *Paul VI*, 489.

suffering, backwardness, and decay.[33] As a result, development programs in Africa—governmental or non-governmental—have been
driven by short-term interventionism rather than wealth creation. In its
analysis of the socio-economic challenges facing Africa, the lineamenta for the Second African Synod wondered why the assets of Africa have remained a source of conflict and exploitation rather than a
means for bringing prosperity to Africa. It states, "Africa's immense
resources are in direct contrast to the misery of its poor. The situation
becomes even more scandalous if consideration is given to the wealth
amassed in the hands of a privileged few."[34]

The assets of Africa—human, cultural, natural, social and religious—have rarely been developed to build lasting and sustainable
practices for human and cosmic flourishing in the continent. The kind
of apocalyptic images of Africa in international appeals for charity—
"helping Africa", "race against time", "the life you can save" in Africa—have resulted in more needs-based interventions rather than facing up to the serious questions about social justice. The churches need
to ask the more fundamental question why there is so much suffering
and poverty among many Africans in a continent with rich human and
natural resources. Why, despite having the most fertile, arable lands in
the world, do about 200 million Africans suffer from chronic hunger?[35]

The final characteristic of these development initiatives is they
work autonomously without coordinating efforts with each other. The
different Christian religious denominations do not often work together
in aid initiatives. Different international organizations in Africa work
like rivals. Rarely do governments work with NGOs, FBOs, and UN
agencies to coordinate such key areas as education, health, and civic
education. There are instances where this has been done, especially in

---

[33] See Overseas Development Institute, "Growth Without Development: Looking
Beyond Inequality, Briefing Paper 47," www.odi.org/sites/odi.org.uk/files/odi-as-
sets/publications-opinion-files/3474.pdf. The authors highlight the impact of
Wolfson's polarization measure compared to Gini's coefficient for explaining inequality in society and why the middle class in the US for instance is shrinking even
though there is a marked increase or growth in wealth. They argue further: "Unlike
the measurement of inequality, polarisation measures focus on the clustering of
members of a society at more than one income level – referred to as poles – capturing convergence around these income levels. Polarisation measures help to clarify
why economic growth does not always translate into human development. They provide a distinct and complementary insight into the link between growth and human
development, capturing the distributional aspects missed by traditional inequality
measures."
[34] Second Special Assembly for Africa, "The Church in Africa in Service to Reconciliation, Justice and Peace," www.vatican.va/roman_curia/synod/docu-
ments/rc_synod_doc_20060627_ii-assembly-africa_en.html.
[35] Ernest Harsch, "Africa Beyond Famine," *Africa Recovery* 17, no. 1 (May 2003):
10.

the battle against HIV/AIDS, but they are often crisis driven rather than well thought out and implemented programs.

The Need to Accurately Understand the Causes of Poverty
The *Lineamenta* of the Second African Synod was very direct and unequivocal in its judgment about the social condition of Africa,

> In most African countries, despite recently achieved progress, the rate of literacy continues to be among the lowest in the world. In many places, the educational system is constantly deteriorating, the health system is in shambles, and social welfare is almost non-existent. With the lack of order, the weak are always the people most threatened. Likewise, in the area of demographics, one can't be silent at the imbalance between a population which is witnessing a record rate of annual growth, and resources which remain unutilized, if not being totally depleted. Africa's immense resources are in direct contrast to the misery of its poor.[36]

Moreover, the life of many Africans today is not better than it was when Pope Paul VI penned *Populorum Progressio* in 1967. The 2012 Human Development Index (HDI) reveals that the 12 countries of the world at the lowest rungs are in Africa. In the 2015 report, 34 of the countries in the low development index are in Africa. According to this report, even though the number of people living in the low HDI fell by nearly 20 million, human deprivations are still widespread and much human potential remain unused. For instance, 11 children under five die every minute; 33 mothers die every hour; and about 37 million people live with HIV and 11 million with tuberculosis; 103 million young people between the ages of 15-24 are illiterate and there are 74 million young people who have no job. These statistics refer especially to Africa where two-thirds of her countries fall in the lowest rungs of the human development index.[37]

The 2015 report which looked at the situation of employment worldwide emphasizes that "people are the real wealth of nations, and human development focuses on enlarging people's choices," especially with regard to building human capabilities.[38] Thus, the greatest asset of Africa is her young people:

---

[36] Second Special Assembly for Africa, "The Church in Africa in Service to Reconciliation, Justice and Peace," www.vatican.va/roman_curia/synod/documents/rc_synod_doc_20060627_ii-assembly-africa_en.html.

[37] United Nations Development Program, *Human Development Report 2015: Work for Human Development* (New York: United Nations Development Program, 2015), 3, 29-30.

[38] United Nations Development Program, *Human Development Report 2015*, 1-2.

> With 200 million people aged between 15-24 (the youth
> bracket), Africa has the youngest population in the world.
> The current trend indicates that this figure will double by
> 2045, according to the 2012 African Economic Outlook re-
> port prepared by experts from the African Development
> Bank (AFDB), the UN Development Program (UNDP),
> and the UN Economic Commission for Africa (ECA) and
> the industrialized Countries' Organization for Economic
> Cooperation and Development (OECD) among others.[39]

The sad news, however, is that, according to the World Bank, 60% of
Africa's young people are jobless.

While many scholars question the accuracy of these statistics,
many of these indicators were noted by the Second African Synod: the
high unemployment rate among young people in Africa, high maternal
and infant mortality, poor health care, poor governance in many African countries, low life expectancy, low standard of living, deteriora-
tion in economic and social conditions, a lack of capacity for mitiga-
tion and adaptation to the effects of climate change, and low levels of
human security. Many African countries suffer from persistent fratri-
cidal wars, ethnic strife, and the pitiable spectacle of refugees and displaced persons.[40] While economic growth is recorded in countries like
South Africa, Botswana, Senegal, and Ghana, it does not translate into
changes in the living conditions of citizens. There is a 30% youth unemployment in Senegal, while 70% of young people in Ghana are either self-employed or keeping themselves busy in working for their
families.[41]

These statistics do not provide an accurate understanding of Africa's poverty. Dayo Olopade argues strongly that African development is following a different trajectory. There is a convergence of interests, creativity, local initiatives, and significant victories and positive stories of young people, women, and civil societies which are
changing the face of Africa, but these factors do not show up on the
clinical development graph of the UN or the World Top Incomes Da-
tabase (WTID). Olopade, therefore, argues that, "When you're thinking of Africa in the context of the wars you've seen, the poverty you

---

[39] Kingsley Ighobor, "Africa's Youth: A 'Ticking Time Bomb' or an Opportunity?"
Africa Renewal 27, no 1. (May 2013): 10-12.
[40] Second Special Assembly for Africa, "The Church in Africa in Service to Reconciliation, Justice and Peace," www.vatican.va/roman_curia/synod/docu-
ments/rc_synod_doc_20060627_ii-assembly-africa_en.html.
[41] Ighobor, "Africa's Youth," 11.

assume, or the government you've given up on, you're likewise missing the point."[42] In his magisterial work, *The Fortunes of Africa*, Martin Meredith argues that,

> The lure of Africa's riches remains as strong in the twenty-first century as in the past. As well as the activities of Western corporations, new players have entered the field. The rising economic might of China and other Asian countries has stimulated a boom in demand for Africa's oil and mineral resources. Land too has become a prized commodity once more…But much of the wealth generated by foreign activity flows out of Africa to destinations abroad. Africa's ruling elites further drain their countries of funds, stashing huge sums in bank accounts and properties abroad.[43]

Meredith argues further that Africa has its own peculiar problems like unreliable rainfall, frequent droughts, harsh and variable climate, challenging terrains, and human and animal diseases.[44] In this light, the analysis of poverty in Africa must begin with an accurate understanding of the conditions facing the continent. Africa cannot be understood in isolation, and the social mission of the Church in Africa must have a correct diagnosis of the African social context.

The Need to Include Women

One area of the social mission of the Church in Africa which carries so much promise is harvesting the gifts of African woman. The question of the role of women and gender equity is strongly raised in Pope Benedict XVI's *Africae Munus*, as it was in the deliberations of the October 2009 Synod. Benedict writes, "The Church has the duty to contribute to the recognition and liberation of women, following the example of Christ's own esteem for them…." (no. 7).[45] However, papal documents have struggled to develop ethical principles which could promote and protect the rights of women. According to Henriot,

> As several feminist scholars have pointed out, this may be the result of an emphasis on "proper nature" and "proper role" of woman—seeming to imply that women have a

---

[42] Dayo Olopade, *The Bright Continent: Breaking Rules and Making Change in Modern Africa* (Boston: Houghton Mifflin Harcourt, 2014), 13-14.

[43] Martin Meredith, *The Fortunes of Africa: A 5000-Year History of Wealth, Greed and Endeavor* (New York: Public Affairs, 2014), xvii.

[44] Meredith, *The Fortunes of Africa*, xvii.

[45] I am grateful to Pete Henriot for sharing with me the original draft of his article where he analyzed *Africae Munus* and did a creative appropriation and critique of this document. I also owe to Pete a lot of inspiration for his pioneering work of social analysis within the Catholic social teaching tradition, and his activist work in Africa in Zambia, and now in Malawi.

"nature" distinct from men's. As a result, insufficient attention is paid both to the massive contributions made by
women to economic development (e.g. food production
and health care) and social development (e.g. , education),
and to the massive obstacles they face (e.g. suffering dis-
proportionately from poverty, illiteracy and malnutri-
tion).[46]

The Church must support the rights and dignity of women more effectively. As Musimbi R. A. Kanyoro writes,

The witness of the Church in Africa will not be credible
unless the Church takes into account the traumatic situation
of the millions of women and the perilous conditions of the
outcast of our societies. What meaning can faith have in
churches that seek to be liberated without sharing the people's battles with the forces of oppression assaulting their
dignity? ...These questions frighten churches and communities with long established traditions and practices of injustices to women. They threaten our institutional comfort
as churches, our invested privileges, our secure situations
and they threaten the security of our judgment of what is
right and what is wrong.[47]

The subjugation and marginalization of women is deeply rooted in
various patriarchal ethos and has contributed to the violation of
women's rights in Africa. In Africa about 51% of African women have
been victims of violence, 11% suffer violence during pregnancy, 21%
marry before the age of fifteen and 24% experience genital mutilation.[48] The various forms of female abuse include domestic violence,
ritual bride price, forced marriages, sexual harassment, punitive wid-
owhood rites, female genital mutilation, rape, prostitution, and en-
forcement of gender-biased laws. These oppressive practices deface
the dignity of the African woman and are exacerbated by the consequences arising from the socio-religious, economic, and political
realms. As a result, the life of an African woman unfolds along the
trajectory of vassalage: at home she serves every member of the family; in society she has limited opportunities; in the culture she is a victim of traditions.[49]

---

[46] Peter Henriot, "Who Cares About Africa?" 229.

[47] Musimbi R. A. Kanyoro, *Introducing Feminist Cultural Hermeneutics: An African Perspective* (Ohio: Pilgrim Press, 2002), 80.

[48] See Anne Arabome, "Woman, You Are Set Free! Women and Discipleship in the
Church," in *Reconciliation, Justice, and Peace: The Second African Synod*, ed.
Agbonkhianmeghe E. Orobator (New York: Orbis, 2011), 119.

[49] Arabome, "Woman, You Are Set Free! Women and Discipleship in the Church,"
120.

Even in this situation, women are still active participants in the economy. According to a survey of nine African countries by the Food and Agriculture Organization (FAO) in 1996, about 80% of the economically active female labor force is employed in agriculture. Food production is the major activity of rural women, and their responsibilities and labor inputs often exceed those of men in most areas in Africa. Women also provide much of the labor for men's cultivation of export crops from which they derive little benefits. Women are responsible for 70% of food production, 50% of domestic food storage, 100% of food processing, 50% of animal husbandry, and 60% of agricultural marketing.[50]

In my work with the Canadian Samaritans for Africa in over twelve women asset-based projects in four African countries, I have seen how the conditions of women can change with solidarity and participatory practices. African women do not need handouts; they need the Church and state to remove patriarchal obstacles which prevent them from entrepreneurial activities like owning land or running and maintaining a bank account without a male co-signer.

CONCLUSION

The goal of this essay is to show the enduring significance of *Populorum Progressio* for Africa and those factors hindering the development for which it calls. For these challenges to be overcome, the Church needs to become an evangelizing community that, according to Pope Francis, is "involved by word and deed in people's daily lives," "standing by them," "touching their suffering," and "bearing fruits in their lives" (*Evangelii Gaudium*, no. 24). This is similar to the message of Paul VI that the reversal of history to conform to the will of God for the world will require not only the enunciation of sound social doctrine but daily practices by all, especially the poor, in bringing about justice and peace in the world. M

---

[50] Takyiwaa Manuh, "Women in Africa's Development," *Africa Recovery* 11 (April 1998): www.un.org/en/africarenewal/bpaper/maineng.htm.

Vulnerability and Development: Rereading *Populorum Progressio* in Light of Feminicide

Marianne Tierney FitzGerald

IFTY YEARS AGO, *Populorum Progressio* highlighted the importance of caring for the developing world and asserted the significance of social justice. The document was addressed to the Catholic community but also called upon those outside of the Church—"men of deep thought and wisdom—Catholics and Christians, believers in God and devotees of truth and justice, all men of good will" (no. 83)—to be aware of the challenges around the world. Despite the fact that Pope Paul VI called for change, many of the issues raised in *Populorum Progressio* are still with us today. Challenges of food scarcity, clean water, and access to education are all immediate problems that need to be addressed in many areas of the world. Pope Paul VI drew attention to the plight of those in the developing world and focused on issues that still resonate with us today. One modern issue *Populorum Progressio* does not address is the problem of feminicide, or the misogynistic killing of women by men, perhaps because the issue had not yet received the attention and concern which it generates today. Even though feminicide is not discussed in *Populorum Progressio*, this article will argue that, by engaging the important themes of integral human development and poverty, *Populorum Progressio* can advance an understanding that feminicide threatens the full personhood of women and that insistence on integral human development creates an imperative for the Church to do more to support the dignity and value of women.

INTEGRAL HUMAN DEVELOPMENT IN *POPULORUM PROGRESSIO*

Populorum Progressio provides an examination of integral human development and explores what it means to be fully human. Pope Paul VI wrote about the importance of recognizing the full personhood of each individual and ensuring that human rights were respected and upheld. Today, we need to hear this call again since our world continues to struggle to protect human rights and defend the integrity of the marginalized.

Throughout *Populorum Progressio*, Paul VI identifies ways in which the global community must respect and promote the integral personhood of individuals, particularly in the developing world. He says, "The ultimate goal is full-bodied humanism. And does this not mean the fulfillment of the whole man and of every man?" (no. 42) *Populorum Progressio* identifies the basic human needs of all individuals and asks that not only the Catholic community but also "all men of good will" (no. 83) consider those whose circumstances force them to live on the margins. Pope Paul stresses that "there can be no progress towards the complete development of man without the simultaneous development of all humanity in the spirit of solidarity" (no. 43). By calling on the established principle of solidarity, he emphasizes the idea that people are interdependent and necessarily rely on one another. Those in the developed world ought to stand with those on the margins in meaningful ways. Moreover, "all of humanity" would seem to include women as well as men in the imperative to work for the development of all.

The idea of integral humanism in *Populorum Progressio* includes making sure that fundamental needs are provided for and protected. For example, Pope Paul VI decries the fact that many in the world are without food. He notes that it is impossible to be "unaware of the fact that on some continents countless men and women are ravished by hunger and countless numbers of children are undernourished.... Thus whole populations are immersed in pitiable conditions and lose heart" (no. 45). Food is only one example. Paul VI makes clear that ensuring "life's necessities" is the bare minimum for achieving "truly human conditions" (no. 21).

The full development of the human person is contingent upon each individual having access to the resources that are available. Pope Paul asserts that "every man has the right to glean what he needs from the earth" (no. 22). He goes on to say that wealthier nations have a responsibility to support nations that are still struggling to develop. The document states, "the superfluous goods of wealthier nations ought to be placed at the disposal of poorer nations" (no. 49) in order to create a more just distribution of wealth and resources. This global imbalance of resources created situations of injustice, and the pope used his document to call on the leaders of the developed world to share their wealth and power more generously.

FEMINICIDE IN MEXICO, GUATEMALA, AND HONDURAS

Although feminicide is a phenomenon that can be found around the world, for the purpose of this analysis, our focus will be restricted to three countries of Latin America: Mexico, Guatemala, and Honduras. The statistics regarding incidences of violence against women in these countries are staggering. While each serves as its own individual case study, at least three commonalities relate to the high levels of violence against women in this part of the world.

First, in all three countries, a significant number of women work in *maquiladoras*, or factories, producing goods for export. The working conditions found within *maquiladoras* are often detrimental to human flourishing and fail to promote an environment of respecting human dignity. Ciudad Juárez, a major border city in Mexico, is home to many *maquiladoras* where women work long hours for very little pay. Many of these *maquiladoras* are located on the outskirts of cities and the (overwhelmingly male) managers arrange shifts that require women to either come in very early in the morning or leave in the middle of the night, which puts them at risk. Women, for the most part, have not been invited to participate in the conversations about what would be safer for them, so they continue to work in dangerous situations. The *maquiladoras* employ hundreds of women who are often seen as nothing more than pieces on an assembly line that can be easily replaced if they go missing. The rise of *maquiladoras* in the wake of NAFTA (the North American Free Trade Agreement) in 1994 has corresponded to the high numbers of women being killed in Latin America. Women are rarely in positions of leadership within the *maquiladoras* and have subsequently been placed at risk.

Pope Paul VI, in *Populorum Progressio*, writes of the importance of work that offers one a sense of dignity. He quotes Pope John XXIII who "stressed the urgent need of restoring dignity to the worker and making him a real partner in the common task" (no. 28). Although factories in Latin America offer women an opportunity to work, the work in which they are engaged is not work that restores their dignity or recognizes their full humanity. Women are often seen as little more than the objects they are working to create and their voices are often ignored. *Maquiladora* culture and the ways in which women's voices have been discounted have both contributed to growing rates of gender-based violence.

The second factor contributing to the high level of violence across these three Latin America countries is the dominant cultures of *machismo* and *marianismo*. *Machismo* refers to a general attitude of "manliness" that includes misogyny and a domination of women. Scholars Karen Englander, Carmen Yáñez, and Xochitl Barney define *machismo* as "a term used for the performance of masculinity in many contemporary, international contexts and it is used as a descriptor of unwelcome male behavior."[1] They also note that "the extreme form [of *machismo*] is manifested as hate and extreme physical and psychological violence against women and it has been reported in a number

---

[1] Karen Englander, Carmen Yáñez and Xochitl Barney, "Doing Science within a Culture of Machismo and Marianismo," *Journal of International Women's Studies* 13, no. 3 (2012): 68.

of Latin American countries to differing degrees by the United Nations specialist on violence against women."[2]

While men in Latin America feel the need to prove their manhood, women are frequently culturally forced to be meek and submissive, in a posture of *marianismo*. *Marianismo* refers to the idea of adopting an attitude of meekness that resembles the prevalent cultural portrayal of the Blessed Virgin Mary. Englander, Yáñez, and Barney describe *marianismo* as "performed through a collection of behaviors that are ascribed as positive."[3] This type of cultural norm leads women to be obedient and subservient, especially to their husbands or authoritative men. Women are expected to be "spiritually and morally superior to men" but also "self-negating and martyrs for their children."[4]

The dual problem of men being especially misogynistic and women being submissive leads to skewed societal roles and norms. As these attitudes have become ingrained in society, they have become harder to undo. It has become commonplace for men to be violent or just patronizing towards women. At the same time, women are seen as less important members of society and are considered to be generally more disposable. Their voices matter less than men's. These attitudes have contributed to high rates of feminicide throughout Latin America. Due to the culture of *machismo* and *marianismo* throughout Latin America, women are oppressed and economically restrained. It is therefore often necessary for women to get whatever jobs they can, despite the fact that jobs in *maquiladoras* often put them at risk.

In keeping with prior teachings on the nature of humanity, Pope Paul VI does not differentiate between genders in *Populorum Progressio*. Reading the document, we can infer that he affirms the full personhood of women as well as men since he does not make gender distinctions and often emphasizes the plight of all of humanity. Throughout *Populorum Progressio*, he advocates on behalf of the marginalized and those who are suffering without regard to gender or other factors. He writes of the importance of recognizing the dignity of all persons and a desire for peace as well as the fulfillment of the common good. The institutional violence that has been inflicted on women in places like Mexico, Guatemala, and Honduras is not in keeping with the integral development of the human person or the development of the common good as understood in *Populorum Progressio*. Pope Paul, in 1967, asserted, "We must make haste. Too many people are suffering" (no. 29). Unfortunately, the actions that the pope advocated for have not come to pass. Although some progress has been made, changes have been slow and often ineffective.

[2] Englander, Yáñez and Barney, "Doing Science," 68.
[3] Englander, Yáñez and Barney, "Doing Science," 69.
[4] Englander, Yáñez and Barney, "Doing Science," 69.

Finally, the growing drug trade throughout Latin America has contributed to the high rate of feminicide in Mexico, Guatemala, and Honduras. Drug culture and the social and political influence of *narcotraficantes,* or drug lords, have led to the increased prevalence of criminal gangs. As gangs have taken control of neighborhoods, violence has inevitably spiked, and more women have become victims of violent gang rituals and sexual violence. Women have also been affected by gang violence because many women have been coerced into joining neighborhood gangs. Their participation in these kinds of activities increases their risk of being targeted by rival gang members. In addition to participating directly in gang violence, women in Mexico, Guatemala, and Honduras have been accidentally caught in the middle of drug or gang activity.

In 2012, *The New York Times* interviewed Hector Hawley, who was responsible for investigating and documenting many of the crime scenes where women had been killed in Ciudad Juárez, Mexico. Hawley said that these women were "a more vulnerable group"[5] because of their status in society. He specialized in women's murder cases and, in his view, "the stunning tally of women killed [was] mostly caused by the increased local involvement in gangs and drugs; and jealous men. Often, both gangs and jealousy come together in a single case."[6]

While *maquiladoras, machismo* and *marianismo,* and the drug trade contribute to the violence against women, exploring the particular situations in Mexico, Guatemala and Honduras provides a more comprehensive understanding of what feminicide looks like in Latin America. These three countries are not the only places where feminicide is occurring, but they are among the countries in the developing world where the rates of violence against women have been the highest. There are specific reasons why feminicide has emerged as a concern in these three countries, although statistics show that feminicide is also a prominent issue in El Salvador and Colombia.[7] These statistics indicate that in Mexico, Guatemala, and Honduras, women's safety and security are constantly at risk and so women in these countries are seen as disposable individuals whose lives matter less.

In Ciudad Juárez, in the state of Chihuahua, Mexico, the reality of feminicide has been impossible to ignore. Feminicide has, in recent years, become part of the identity of the city because of the growing

---

[5] Damien Cave, "Wave of Violence Swallows More Women in Juárez," *The New York Times,* www.nytimes.com/2012/06/24/world/americas/wave-of-violence-swallows-more-women-in-juarez-mexico.html.

[6] Cave, "Wave of Violence."

[7] Mimi Yagoub, "Why Does Latin America Have the World's Highest Female Murder Rates?" *InSight Crime: Investigation and Analysis of Organized Crime,* www.insightcrime.org/news-analysis/why-does-latin-america-have-the-world-s-highest-female-murder-rates.

attention paid to the high numbers of murdered women. The international aid organization Amnesty International reported that between 1993 and 2007, approximately 400 women had been killed in Ciudad Juárez.[8] Those figures have continued to grow, although the worst years of feminicide in Ciudad Juárez are considered to be 2009-2010. It has been difficult to get exact numbers on the women who have been killed or who have disappeared from Ciudad Juárez because women do not always get reported as missing and because there is no single resource keeping track of women who have disappeared; sources, however, have said that 304 women were killed in the city in 2010 alone.[9] A *New York Times* article reported that 60 women had been killed in the first six months of 2012, with 18 feminicides in the month of April.[10]

These numbers are shocking, but the stories recounted by families about the casual manner with which authorities respond to these killings and disappearances are even more disturbing. Families report that authorities often fail to investigate the killings at all and may insinuate that the young women in question could have run away to the United States or become prostitutes. They will also imply that the women should not have dressed a particular way or gone out at a certain time of day or night and suggest that the violence that was perpetrated against them was "deserved."[11] There is a sense that there is no accountability for these crimes, and killers know that they will literally get away with murder.

Guatemala's rate of feminicide is also staggering. As in Juárez, there are competing reports on the exact numbers of women who have been killed, but Amnesty International reported in 2007 that there had been 2,500 feminicides since 2001, and 299 between January and May in 2005.[12] These numbers have continued to grow.

The reality of feminicide in Guatemala began during the 36-year civil war in Guatemala from 1960 to 1996. The Council on Hemispheric Affairs reports that during the Guatemalan civil war, "thousands of men were trained to commit acts of gender-based violence.

---

8 United Nations Economic Commission for Latin America and the Caribbean (ECLAC), "No More! The Right of Women to Live a Life Free of Violence in Latin America and the Caribbean," www.unicef.org/lac/No_more.pdf.
9 Cave, "Wave of Violence."
10 Cave, "Wave of Violence."
11 See the Council on Hemispheric Affairs (CHA), "The International Violence Against Women Act: Could IVAWA Save Guatemala from Femicide?" www.coha.org/the-international-violence-against-women-act-could-ivawa-save-guatemala-from-femicide/: "Police and other government officials frequently accuse victims of gang associations, drug abuse, or prostitution; the female victims' physical appearance or attire is often cited as cause for delay or for the failure to investigate and prosecute."
12 ECLAC, "No More!"

When peace was established in 1996, those same men effortlessly re-joined society."[13] An entire generation of men grew up in Guatemala learning about different ways to abuse women as part of their military training, and when the war ended, they could not merely forget what they had learned, and the violence had become "normalized." Currently, "Guatemala continues to bear the mark of the civil war: common methods [of gender violence] include rape, dismemberment, torture, and mutilation, acts reminiscent of tactics used during the war."[14] This history of the civil war in Guatemala contributes to a culture where women, especially indigenous women, are not valued as highly as men are and where violence is an everyday occurrence.

Despite attempts to restore peace in Guatemala in the aftermath of the civil war, violence has continued to dictate Guatemalan life. The Guatemalan military has been accused (and in some cases convicted) of carrying out massacres in the villages of indigenous peoples in the northern part of the country during the civil war.[15] The genocide that the military carried out often included raping groups of indigenous women before killing them or leaving them to be humiliated in their villages. The practice of rape as a tool of war was fully utilized during the Guatemalan civil war, which has been documented in the truth and reconciliation commissions.[16] Even though peace has existed for many

---

[13] CHA, "The International Violence Against Women Act."

[14] CHA, "The International Violence Against Women Act."

[15] Several former Guatemalan Army commanders are in prison because of their involvement in massacres during the Guatemalan civil war. See Dan Whitcomb, "Ex-Guatemalan Army Office Tied to Massacre Sentenced to U.S. Prison," *Reuters*, www.reuters.com/article/2014/02/10/us-usa-guatemala-massacre-idUSBREA1920H20140210. In 2013, Gen. Efraín Ríos Montt was found guilty of genocide and crimes against humanity. See Elisabeth Malkin, "Former Leader of Guatemala is Guilt of Genocide Against Mayan Group," *The New York Times*, www.nytimes.com/2013/05/11/world/americas/gen-efrain-rios-montt-of-guatemala-guilty-of-genocide.html. A higher court in Guatemala, however, overturned the guilty verdict based on a technicality and ordered a retrial, which has not yet taken place. The general feeling among Guatemalans is that the guilty verdict is still true. See Kelly McEvers' interview with Pamela Yates, "Guatemalan Ex-Dictator Rios Montt Found Mentally Unfit for Genocide Retrial," *National Public Radio*, www.npr.org/2015/07/08/421225062/guatemalan-ex-dictator-rios-montt-found-mentally-unfit-for-genocide-retrial. In this interview, filmmaker Pamela Yates says that, according to many Guatemalans, there is a saying: "la sentencia esta vigente – the verdict is valid. He was judged to be a genocidaire, and in their minds, he is a genocidaire."

[16] Rachel Hatcher, "Truth and Forgetting in Guatemala: An Examination of *Memoria del Silencio* and *Nunca Más*." *Canadian Journal of Latin American and Caribbean Studies*, 34, no. 67 (2009): 131-162. Following the Peace Accords in Guatemala in 1996, the Guatemalan state launched a project attempting to uncover the truth of what had happened during the war. The state project is known (in English) as the Commission for the Clarification of History or CEH (Comisión para el Esclarecimiento Historico). At the same time, the Catholic Church created its own

years and both the political community and the Catholic Church have tried to heal the country by establishing truth commissions, the legacy of violence, especially gender-based violence, remains and patterns of feminicide have become a reality.

In Honduras, incidences of feminicide have emerged in the country since the 2009 coup d'état that left the state of Honduras insecure and unstable.[17] As a result of this instability, the rate of feminicide in Honduras has risen sharply in the last seven years. One report by the Mesoamerican Initiative of Human Rights Defenders states that feminicides in Honduras have risen by 62% since 2009. And the *Observatorio de la Violencia* or "Violence Observatory" at the National Autonomous University of Honduras has said that at least one woman was killed every 13 hours in 2013, resulting in 629 feminicides.[18]

Since 2009, Honduras has been sharply divided between those who supported the former president Manuel "Mel" Zelaya, and those who supported the coup and the newly-elected president Porfirio "Pepe" Lobo. Because of this disruption, Honduras has become extremely violent. Zelaya was largely considered a leftist president, which contributed to his ouster, in addition to the speculation that he was planning to illegally extend his presidency. While he was president, he supported the development of women's groups and defended women's education programs. He raised the minimum wage significantly and provided funding for programs that were judged by more right-wing politicians to be "too socialist." As a result of his policies, many women and *campesinas,* or women who live in rural areas, supported Zelaya and opposed the coup. These women have not remained silent about what they feel was a violation of their constitutional rights. They have continued to speak out against the coup and regularly taken political action.

Because many members of the police force, which is largely a military-run police, do not approve of the political activism of women in Honduras, they have participated in practices of feminicide and violence against women. Stories have emerged of women being killed by police because of their participation in democratic demonstrations and protests, and in other situations women have been assaulted based on their political involvement.[19] It has been reported that in the months

---

commission called the Recuperation of Historical Memory Project or REMHI (Recuperación de la Memoria Histórica.) These works were titled *Memoria del Silencio* and *Nunca Más* and they were published in February1999 and April 1998.

[17] Elisabeth Malkin, "Honduran President is Ousted in Coup," *The New York Times,* June 6, 2009, www.nytimes.com/2009/06/29/world/americas/29honduras.html.

[18] Dan Beeton, "The Legacy Children of the Honduran Coup," *Al Jazeera America,* america.aljazeera.com/opinions/2014/6/violence-in-hondurasunaccompaniedminorsimmigrationtous.html.

[19] For example, coup protester Irma Villanueva was at a demonstration in August 2009 when she was arrested by police officers along with other demonstrators. She

following the 2009 coup, police and military forces targeted those who supported Zelaya as well as progressive radio stations, news outlets, and women who continued to protest and fight for their constitutional rights to be reinstated.[20] In Honduras, women are already especially at risk because of their social vulnerability, and, in 2013, a United Nations report stated that Honduras has the highest murder rate in the world.[21] Feminicide in Honduras could continue to escalate to a level that is similar to what it has been in Ciudad Juárez if it continues to go unchecked.

In Mexico, Guatemala, and Honduras, feminicide is an all too common occurrence. These deaths occur regularly and in too many cases, no one does anything about it. Scholar Hilda Morales Trujillo has noted the danger that comes with this complacency. She says, "The wave of misogynist violence has yet to provoke outright indignation among civil society. Beyond the organized women's movement and a few other exceptions, civil society remains unperturbed by these acts."[22] Women's communities are necessary because they highlight the only places in society where these women are not disappearing into obscurity completely. Women need to be valued as full members of society and not just replaceable parts of an economic system. The human dignity of all women needs to be honored in order for anything to really change in Latin America.

POPULORUM PROGRESSIO AND FEMINICIDE

In *Populorum Progressio*, Pope Paul VI advocated and explained the notion of integral human development and its applications to the perceived problems of the time. The nations of the developing world were asserting their autonomy after a long legacy of colonialism yet hampered by their disadvantaged status within the global economy.

---

was taken away from the protest and beaten and raped by four police officers. She told her story on the Jesuit-run radio station Radio Progreso. See Robert Naiman, "Coup Protester Gang-Raped by Honduran Police," *Just Foreign Policy*, www.justforeignpolicy.org/node/304. The testimony of Irma Villanueva was documented by the Inter-American Commission on Human Rights. Human Rights Watch announced a report generated by the Inter-American Commission on Human Rights (IACHR) on August 25, 2009 which said that "women [in Honduras] were especially subject to acts of violence and humiliation because of their gender." See "Honduras: Rights Report Shows Need for Increased International Pressure: Widespread and Continuing Abuses Documented by Inter-American Commission," *Human Rights Watch*, www.hrw.org/en/news/2009/08/25/honduras-rights-report-shows-need-increased-international-pressure.

[20] Dana Frank, "The Thugocracy Next Door," *Politico Magazine*, www.politico.com/magazine/story/2014/02/honduras-the-thugocracy-ext-door103883.html.

[21] Frank, "Thugocracy Next Door."

[22] Hilda Morales Trujillo, "Femicide and Sexual Violence in Guatemala," in *Terrorizing Women: Feminicide in the Américas*, eds. Rosa Linda Fregoso and Cynthia L. Bejarano (North Carolina: Duke University Press, 2010), 135.

Populorum Progressio is addressed to the problems faced by the developing nations of Paul's own time, and yet its vision of integral human development remains relevant for the emerging problems of our own day. Although many of the problems noted by Pope Paul persist, such as poverty, hunger, and unequal trade relations, his vision of integral human development can also be fruitfully applied to the issue of feminicide.

Feminicide is defined as "the misogynist killing of women by men"[23] with impunity. The phenomenon of feminicide has only been explored academically within the last thirty years or so.[24] Feminicide is a radical obstruction to integral human development. The systematic patterns of feminicide in places such as Mexico, Guatemala, and Honduras indicate that the human dignity of women is often ignored and that women are seen as disposable members of society, which places them as some of the most marginalized of people within some societies. Women are incapable of thriving and holistically developing if they are living in fear and unable to access the resources they need. Patterns of feminicide have threatened women's ability to maintain employment, since many women have been killed while traveling to and from work, as well as their ability to participate fully in activities of leisure, such as going out at night. Feminicide prevents women in Mexico, Guatemala, and Honduras from being able to live fully human lives and inhibits their ability to embrace their full personhood.

Rereading *Populorum Progressio* with feminicide in mind can highlight ways in which the document has the potential to speak to this troubling issue, as well as its limitations. *Populorum Progressio* does an excellent job of portraying the struggles and challenges of pursuing economic and social justice. The document discusses the violence of poverty and the suffering of those who are forced to live on the margins, but it does not highlight the fact that the majority of those living in poverty are women. This may be because attention had not yet been brought to this issue, and data on the feminization of poverty was not available until well after 1967, with the first studies on this issue not published until 1978, the last year of Paul VI's pontificate.[25] With

---

[23] Jill Radford and Diana E.H. Russell, eds., *Femicide: The Politics of Woman Killing* (New York: Twayne Publishers, 1992), xi.

[24] The term "femicide" was first introduced into the academy in 1976 by Canadian anthropologists Diana E.H. Russell and Jill Radford. In the 1990's, with their permission, it was adapted to "feminicide" by Mexican anthropologist Marcela Lagarde. See Monica A. Maher, "Daring to Dream: Faith and Feminicide in Latin America," *Weep Not for Your Children: Essays on Religion and Violence*, eds. Lisa Isherwood and Rosemary Radford Ruether (New York: Routledge, 2008), 188.

[25] In 1978, scholar Diana Pearce first talked about the feminization of poverty in her article, "The Feminization of Poverty: Women, Work and Welfare" in *The Urban and Social Change Review: Special Issue on Women and Work* 11, nos. 1-2 (1978): 28-36.

much greater research into this issue and much data accumulated, to-day we are aware that up to 70% of the world's poor are women.[26] Women living in poverty face undue burdens and struggle with issues that do not concern men, including their physical safety.

In addition, *Populorum Progressio* named many of the structures and conditions that have allowed the problems of women in poverty to continue and even worsen. The countries around the world where the rates of violence against women are the highest are also countries where many of the citizens live in poverty.[27] Pope Paul VI wrote that "the disparity between rich and poor nations [would] increase rather than diminish" and that "the rich nations are progressing with rapid strides while the poor nations move forward at a slow pace." (no. 8) This has shown itself to be true in the three countries examined in this article, and the conditions associated with this reality have contributed to the higher numbers of women murdered throughout the developing world. In the same way that the development of all peoples must be a concern for all individuals, the eradication and prevention of feminicide must also be a major concern, as the incidence of feminicide and the conditions which give rise to it are a serious impediment to the integral development of all human beings, as well as the economic development of the nations. *Populorum Progressio* illuminates the Church's concern for those on the margins and calls for solidarity with those who are in real need, and endangered women are among the neediest people on the planet.

In *Populorum Progressio*, Paul made clear that integral human development could not fully be promoted unless the inequalities, social turmoil, and violence at its root were addressed. Although some progress has been made in some areas of the world, the conditions that Paul VI observed are just as true today, and, in the case of feminicide, this means addressing the political corruption and drug trade which have become so prevalent in Mexico and Central America. The drug trade has also contributed to a rise in gang violence as well as shifting cultural norms. Any effort to combat feminicide must address these broader social and cultural issues.

The encyclical can also speak to the need to eradicate this particular gender-based violence through its call for all individuals to participate in the work of promoting human development. Pope Paul VI says that "the Church asks each and every man to hear his brother's plea

---

[26] United Nations Development Programme, "Human Development Report 1995," hdr.undp.org/sites/default/files/reports/256/hdr_1995_en_complete_nostats.pdf.
[27] UN documentation shows that the regions of the world where the rates of feminicide are highest in Latin America and Sub-Saharan Africa. See UNICEF, "Gender and Health," www.unicef.org/esaro/7310_Gender_and_health.html and The United Nations Security General, "Campaign to End Violence Against Women," www.un.org/en/women/endviolence/.

and answer it lovingly" (no. 3). Despite its unfortunately gendered language, which is a product of a different time, Paul here presents us with a universal call to action. Since women in developing countries are even more vulnerable than men, women need to be given a preferential concern when promoting human development. The universal call to action is helpful and serves as an important way that the Church can make a significant difference regarding violence against women. Not only does it serve as a call for all people to become involved in combatting violence against women, but it also suggests that women should take a leading role in asserting the dignity and value of their sisters around the world.

The interconnectedness of humanity and the importance of participation from everyone are major themes of *Populorum Progressio*. "The world situation," writes Pope Paul VI, "requires the concerted effort of everyone, a thorough examination of every facet of the problem—social, economic, cultural and spiritual" (no. 13). This sense of interconnectedness will also be necessary for eradicating feminicide. A cultural shift is necessary in order to dismantle the dominant *machismo* and the embedded norms which have been harmful for women in many areas of the world, especially those that could be classified as "under-developed." The call that Pope Paul VI makes to reach out beyond borders serves as a call to care for women around the world and to work to undo the violence that has been and continues to be perpetrated against women. Partnerships, alliances, and international networks must be strengthened in order to make a violence-free world a more concrete reality. This will require concerted effort and strong advocacy, both endorsed by *Populorum Progressio*. Realizing our own interconnectedness requires participation on behalf of everyone *from* everyone, an important theme that Pope Paul VI returns to throughout *Populorum Progressio*. This concept is one that is perhaps more critical today than it was in 1967, as we are more aware of the conditions of our brothers and sisters in developing countries.

Throughout *Populorum Progressio*, Pope Paul VI is determined to have those in the developed world respond to the developing world in a spirit of solidarity. He says that we must find ways to grow in "friendly relationships of true solidarity that are based on juridical and political equality" (no. 52). The kind of solidarity that Pope Paul believes is necessary for supporting the developed world is the same kind of solidarity that is needed in order to end feminicide, both in Latin America and around the world. People in the developed world have a responsibility to stand with women and activists and do what is necessary to end this epidemic. The spirit of solidarity that is present within *Populorum Progressio* is needed in order to address feminicide in Mexico, Guatemala, and Honduras. In the same way that Pope Paul VI acknowledges that there are challenges to creating a sense of solidarity in the world, there are many obstacles to developing a true sense

of solidarity with those suffering from the effects of feminicide. Without being physically present in these countries and seeing first-hand
the realities of life there, it is difficult to place ourselves in full solidarity. However, as Pope Paul VI advocated for a "heightened sense
of solidarity," so we too are called to recognize the violation of rights
and the human dignity stripped away from those victims of feminicide
and speak out on their behalves.

These issues are only a few of the major themes Pope Paul VI addresses in *Populorum Progressio* which are relevant to those struggling to eradicate feminicide in Mexico, Guatemala, and Honduras,
but they highlight the most important of the imperatives involved: the
connection between physical safety and the possibility of full and integral human development for all people. Although Pope Paul VI does
not address the issue of feminicide directly in *Populorum Progressio*,
his sensitivity to those who are struggling in the face of economic
hardship provides an important bridge to thinking about how Catholic
social teaching can more concretely respond to gender-based violence
and feminicide. Despite Paul VI's use of gender exclusive language
and lack of focus on the intersection of gender and poverty—both in-
dicative of his historical location—many of the ideas he generates can
be translated to discuss women's issues.

LIMITS OF THE CATHOLIC RESPONSE

Despite these promising themes in *Populorum Progressio*, the
Church in Latin America's response to feminicide has been inade-
quate.[28] A re-reading of *Populorum Progressio* highlights the fact that
the Church, both as an institution and as a people, must become more
active in ending feminicide. Women who are living in poverty in
places like Mexico, Guatemala, and Honduras have been unduly burdened by poverty, which brings with it not only the indignities of the
struggle for basic necessities but also the threat to their physical lives
as a result of their social location. *Populorum Progressio* stands in

---

[28] Guatemalan scholar Carlos Aldana Mendoza has written about how the Catholic
Church in Guatemala is actually complicit in feminicide because it has not spoken
out against the violence. See Carlos Aldana Mendoza, "Churches and Faith Communities in the Face of Oppression and Violence Against Indigenous and Mestiza
Women in Guatemala," actalliance.org/wp-content/uploads/2015/09/ Churches-and-
Faith-Communities-in-the-face-of-Oppression-and-Violence-against-Indigenous-
and-Mestiza-Women-in-Guatemala.pdf. American scholar Monica Maher talks
about how "the churches, like the state, are implicated in these crimes [of femini-
cide] due to the institutional sins of silence, omission, negligence and complicity."
See her "Spiritualties of Social Engagement: Women Resisting Violence in Mexico
and Honduras," *Religion and Politics in America's Borderlands*, ed. Sarah Aza-
ransky (Maryland: Lexington Books, 2013), 128. The only church official who is
known to have mentioned feminicide is Cardinal Oscar Rodríguez Maradiaga, Archbishop of Tegucigalpa, Honduras. He called for an end to feminicide during a Good
Friday Stations of the Cross prayer service in 2015.

continuity with Catholic social teaching's preferential option for the poor, with Pope Paul VI writing that Jesus brings the "Gospel to the poor as a sign of His mission." (no. 12) Poverty increases one's vulnerability, which is evident in the statistical analysis of feminicide occurring in under-developed nations such as those examined here. In this way, we can assert that a Church that cares deeply about the needs of the poor can and should do more to help women who are living amidst the threat of feminicide.

Pope Paul VI asserts that the "Church has never failed to foster the human progress of the nations to which she brings faith in Christ" (no. 12). We can see, however, that the Church could still be doing more to foster human development in countries like Mexico, Guatemala, and Honduras and others where feminicide is widespread. The Church in Latin America serves as a powerful institution throughout the developing world, especially in Latin America. Despite wielding formidable influence, the church has not done enough to support women who are living in fear of feminicide, and it has not done enough to advocate for the changes needed to end this violent reality. There are many concrete steps that the Church could and should take to in order to address this injustice, beginning with placing the eradication of gender-based violence and an end to feminicide firmly on the agenda. People from all parts of the community, from grassroots community organizers to bishops, need to understand how to play their part to change the societal norms that permit the unrestricted and unpunished murders of women. If the Church is truly being called to affirm the common good and to support those who are living on the margins, as Pope Paul VI states that it is (no. 24), then the Church needs to be more active in the work of creating a just society for women as well as men.

The Church needs to take a more proactive role in the struggle against feminicide, and a renewed look at *Populorum Progressio* could offer a fruitful place to begin. In addition to looking at *Populorum Progressio* through the lens of violence against women in order to see what possibilities for action exist, church officials could also incorporate more teaching about this violence into the ecclesial culture. For example, this issue could be the focus of more church-sponsored programs and events, with the position that all human beings are valuable and deserve safety as a basic right front and center. In addition to more regular preaching about the harm of feminicide, the Church could work to end this violence by creating institutional programs that offer women greater autonomy and authority in the community, and the Church could also offer some safe havens for those at particular risk. Educating young people about the virtues stressed in *Populorum Progressio* and other social teachings is also of paramount importance so that a new generation may understand human dignity and value, the importance of respecting all individuals, and the need to support the advancement and development of all people in society. The Church could foster community-building programs and retreats that let people share their experiences with all aspects of this problem, though these could be harder to implement among the poor as labor requires so much of the attention and time of the poor. It could also work more substantially with the Protestant and evangelical churches that are quickly growing throughout Latin America in order to build collaborative efforts to address this problem. The Church could also use its powerful influence within society to make more of a political impact, working with sympathetic politicians, NGOs, and institutions such as the United Nations to strengthen coalitions and work for international cooperation and investment in under-developed countries and areas.

Pope Francis has briefly discussed the dangers of violence against women,[29] but the Church as a worldwide institution, beginning with the Vatican, should make this issue a larger agenda issue. Pope Francis, as a man from a poorer country in the global south, is in an unique position to draw attention to the problem of feminicide. His popularity among Catholics in Latin America means that he would have a receptive audience if he chose to explicitly denounce violence against women. The pastoral function of the papacy is also important, particularly when it comes from a pontiff who is so personally popular. Pope Francis has proven that he is a champion of the poor and marginalized and should consistently offer encouragement and support for women who are vulnerable and seeking justice. His "soft power" could also reshape the conversation about faith-based organizations and activism by supporting the work of women on the ground by publicly recognizing and encouraging their efforts.

CONCLUSION

Pope Paul VI's encyclical *Populorum Progressio* can offer some significant insights that speak to the modern issues of violence against women in the developing world. Although feminicide and the particular harms that make women in poverty especially vulnerable were hidden issues when *Populorum Progressio* was composed, the themes and moral imperatives that Paul VI raised in his encyclical offer fruitful resources for addressing these issues in our time. In keeping with the directives of the encyclical, the issue of feminicide should be addressed by the Church more directly, particularly in Latin America and other areas where women are especially vulnerable. In this way, the influence of *Populorum Progressio* can extend indefinitely, serving as

---

[29] See Philip Pullella, "Pope Condemns Female Mutilation, Domestic Violence Against Women," *Reuters*, www.reuters.com/article/us-pope-mutilation-idUSKBN0LB0JM20150207. These comments did not focus on Latin American women specifically but did discuss the need to protect women in general.

an important starting point and also as a way to assert the importance of human flourishing and support a fully integral human development for all people, especially the most vulnerable.∎

Journal of Moral Theology, Vol. 6, No. 1 (2017): 96-111

Populorum Progressio's Vision in an Unequal World: A Theological Ethical Evaluation from the Global South

Raymond Aina, MSP

P OPULORUM PROGRESSIO FULLY DEVELOPED the vision of the Catholic Church as a global church that has special attention for peoples and nations on the margins of globalization. The encyclical shows the "certain progressive tendencies" Giovanni Battista Montini already exhibited during his episcopacy at Milan.[1] Even if the scathing criticisms Paul VI had for neo-liberal globalization and international economic structures caused some discomfort within the Church and the international community, the holistic vision of human development in *Populorum Progressio* has inspired and deepened Catholic Social Thought since then.

However, is the world any better fifty years after the prophetic words of Paul VI? Who is listening to *Populorum Progressio* today where the global economy serves just 1% of the world's population and neglects much of the Global South?[2] This essay investigates this question in four parts. First, this essay summarizes *Populorum Progressio*'s statement of the economic problem facing the world and, second, Paul VI's responsibility ethics as a response to this problem. Third, the essay traces how subsequent encyclicals shifted *Populorum Progressio*'s emphasis on solidarity as a principle of justice resulting in structural change to a virtue that guides personal change. The final section indicates how *Populorum Progressio*'s emphasis on solidarity as work of justice can help the Global South—using the example of Nigeria.

POPULORUM PROGRESSIO'S STATEMENT OF THE PROBLEM

In *Populorum Progressio*, Paul VI spells out the multidimensional

---

[1] Allan Figueroa Deck, "Commentary on *Populorum progressio* (*On the Development of Peoples*)," in *Modern Catholic Social Teaching: Commentaries and Interpretations*, ed. Kenneth R. Himes, O.F.M. (Washington, DC: Georgetown University Press, 2005), 295.

[2] Deborah Hardoon, Sophia Ayele, and Ricardo Fuentes-Nieva, *An Economy for the 1%: How Privilege and Power in the Economy Drive Extreme Inequality and How This Can Be Stopped* (Oxford: Oxfam International, 2016).

problem of the unequal distribution of wealth. These include impoverished nations, lack of progress by poorer nations, the need for international social justice, and the necessity of socio-economic liberty of former colonies (nos. 4-6). Also, a mono-economy at the mercy of price fluctuation in international markets causes a post-colonial gloom (no. 7). Together, these factors widened the gap between the haves and have-nots, and the result is an obscene inequality with a small minority enjoying the wealth and products of the whole (no. 9).

Against this backdrop, Paul VI articulates the Church's responsibility: "The progressive development of peoples is an object of deep interest and concern to the Church." The Church is most interested in the bottom billion that are "consciously striving for fuller growth" (no. 1). The Church has this responsibility because of her nature as a sacrament of Christ's universal salvation. Due to the universality of her status and mission, she is best primed to offer the international community "a global perspective on man and human realities" (no. 13). *Populorum Progressio's* vision of development is holistic. Authentic development must factor in the transcendental (nos. 14-16). Beyond offering maximal moral expectations,[3] *Populorum Progressio* offers a baseline ethics about human existence: if indeed we are "morally serious persons,"[4] there are human conditions that are morally unacceptable (no. 21).

The encyclical offers two ethical principles from the Catholic Social Tradition to back its assertion. Anchored in Gen. 1:28, the goods of the earth belong to every human being; hence, whatever the earth produces is destined for all human beings. The rights conferred on the citizens of the modern state are subordinated to these principles (no. 22). Accordingly, *Populorum Progressio* advocates for the principles of the common good and the universal destination of goods to evaluate contemporary conditions and to ameliorate socio-economic anomalies. For instance, contrary to unbridled liberalism's claim regarding the right to private property, *Populorum Progressio* indicates that this right is not absolute or unconditional. In fact, there are moral grounds for when certain properties can be expropriated (no. 24).[5] Given widespread violations of the twin principles of the common good and the universal destination of goods, *Populorum Progressio* warns of grave dangers if the world does not make haste to reform and restructure

---

[3] Paul VI calls on all to develop supererogatory and noble "values of love and friendship, of prayer and contemplation" (no. 20).

[4] This term is appropriated from Ian Markham's monograph on religious ethics, *Do Morals Matter?: A Guide to Contemporary Religious Ethics* (Massachusetts: Blackwell, 2007), 181-191.

[5] This papal exhortation appears to have partly inspired the Pontifical Council for Justice and Peace's *Towards a Better Distribution of Land: The Challenge of Agrarian Reform*, as well as certain positions in the *Compendium of the Social Doctrine of the Church*. See *Compendium*, no. 180.

both domestic and international economic systems based on Western-style capitalist economies (nos. 29-30).

In responding to this situation, however, Paul VI asks for "reform, not revolution" (nos. 30-31). He reasons that reforms are not as morally problematic as revolutions which tends to produce as much evils as the ones their promoters want to redress. As Paul VI indicates, we cannot do what is morally evil or what we foresee will bring disproportionate evil consequences: "The evil situation that exists, and it surely is evil, may not be dealt with in such a way that an even worse situation results" (no. 31). Hence, in confronting evil situations, people must not lose their moral sense and prudence.[6] Nevertheless, one can argue that based on the virtue of prudence and our moral sense, *Populorum Progressio* gives a caveat for revolution. Reform is the first line of response. Revolution at times might be a last resort, if certain conditions prevail. "Everyone knows, however, that revolutionary uprisings—*except where there is manifest, longstanding tyranny which would do great damage to fundamental personal rights and dangerous harm to the common good of the country*—engender new injustices, introduce new inequities and bring new disasters" (no. 31, italics added). It seems this statement recognizes the importance of prudence and moral sense in discerning appropriate action in the face of grave evil to both the personal and the common good.

PAUL VI'S RESPONSIBILITY ETHIC

In a 1961 Lenten pastoral, Montini, the future Paul VI, offers a glimpse of his responsibility ethic when considering the ambivalence of science and technology. He argues that, while science and technology increased belief in human liberty, they negatively impacted the moral order by enthroning moral relativism. By exalting human liberty, moral relativism divorced liberty from objective principles, "giving it complete autonomy."[7] On the contrary, contends Montini, the human person is "made up of autonomy and heteronomy. Liberty as an end in itself means a liberty that is irrational and uncontrollable."[8] Reawakening the moral sense of heteronomy is necessary in "developing a strong and healthy humanism, the worthy and sacred use of life or any virile and Christian virtues."[9]

---

[6] For Cardinal Giovanni Battista Montini, the future Paul VI, moral sense means "rational enquiry, and which precedes the formulation of juridical norms by the legislature. It is the sense of equity inherent in the human condition, which claims effective application first, before a formal legal system gives it expression in positive law." Prudence is an intellectual faculty which evaluates human action regarding its goodness or moral evil. See James Walsh, ed. *The Mind of Paul VI: On the Church and the World* (London: Geoffrey Chapman, 1964), 85 n. 2.

[7] Walsch, *The Mind of Paul VI*, 91.

[8] Walsch, *The Mind of Paul VI*, 91.

[9] Walsch, *The Mind of Paul VI*, 93.

This heteronomous dimension of the human person offers the ground for a responsibility ethic which Paul VI articulates in *Populorum Progressio*. Paul VI understands responsibility as centering on human ability to be an active moral agent, one with the sense and capacity to contribute to the growth of one's self-worth (no. 9). Personal responsibility therefore is a sense of obligation within a person to better one's worth and surrounding without waiting for an external compulsion. This sense means a movement away from a herd-mentality (no. 6). In no. 15, Paul VI offers his understanding of person-centered responsibility: "In God's plan, every man is born to seek self-fulfillment, for every human life is called to some task by God."

Populorum Progressio demonstrates even today that a "responsibility ethic" can be relational, inclusive and articulated in pluralist societies in ways that make the ethic reasonable to many. This is possible if one locates the source of responsibility in heteronomy. Hence, the call of responsibility from heteronomy is an expression of devotion to God since responsibility calls us to be devoted to the Other-as-Neighbor (no. 42). This call of responsibility suddenly breaks the Cartesian illusion that the autonomous subject is the master and possessor of her/his world.

This sense of responsibility implies that the provocation to action comes from another who "breathes the spirit for action," an *in-spiration* into the self. Heteronomous responsibility therefore is a moral obligation to action that issues from another (God, human persons) and not the self. This contrasts with autonomous responsibility. Heteronomous responsibility recognizes a truth that the autonomous subject is not entirely sovereign. All initiatives for action do not come from the self. The initiatives come from others through their interruptive encounters with the moral subject, who is then compelled to respond accordingly, either proactively or by choosing to turn a blind eye to the imperative of encounter. So, inter-human ethics has its starting point in the "strict heteronomy of the 'inconvenient' appearance of the other."[10] In other words, the unsolicited and undesired appearance of the other is the source of the responsibility of solidarity and justice.

Paul VI demonstrates his understanding of heteronomous responsibility when he states that the responsibility he puts forth is not egocentric; it does not preclude others. On the contrary, personal obligation for self-realization is tied to the human community (no. 17). Every person has a moral obligation to contribute to the development of all persons regardless of their locations and identities. This sense of responsibility is universal and not rooted in particularity. It is a movement towards self-transcendence. Beyond the primordial care for the

---

[10] Roger Burggraeve, *Each Other's Keeper?: Essays on Ethics and the Biblical Wisdom of Love* (Thrissur, India: Marymatha Publications, 2009), 63.

self, we realize in our journey through life that we cannot narrow human responsibility to self-care and self-interest – even in its positive sense.

Paul VI is telling us that there is another level of responsibility, which we discover "accidentally" and unplanned. It is not part of our original existential project. It comes from an "interruptive encounter", like the one lying half-dead on the wayside (cf. Luke 10.30-37). A person's attempt at self-fulfillment is impossible without attentiveness to the other. This is a fundamental movement of responsibility: due to our capacity to be ethically moved, one's being in a world in need of authentic development does not leave one unaffected. Even if one is not culpable, encountering the vulnerability of others demands an ethical response to do something positive about this vulnerability and its source.

This moral obligation to promote authentic progress goes by the name of "solidarity": "We are the heirs of earlier generations, and we reap benefits from the efforts of our contemporaries; we are under obligation to all men. Therefore we cannot disregard the welfare of those who will come after us to increase the human family. The reality of human solidarity brings us not only benefits but also obligations" (no. 17). This sense of responsibility is key for Paul VI's principal plea that the wealthier nations and persons should allow themselves to be ethically moved by the tears and cries of the "wretched of the earth": "Genuine progress does not consist in wealth sought for personal comfort or for its own sake; rather it consists in an economic order designed for the welfare of the human person, where the daily bread that each man receives reflects the glow of brotherly love and the helping hand of God" (no. 86).

JOHN PAUL II'S RECEPTION OF *POPULORUM PROGRESSIO*

In *Sollicitudo Rei Socialis*, which commemorates *Populorum Progressio*'s twentieth anniversary, John Paul II shares a similar diagnosis of social disorders as Paul VI. The problem is the unequal distribution of the means of subsistence destined for universal enjoyment. This inequality has gone beyond localized conflicts between workers and the employers of labor. The social question about an economy of exclusion is posed globally (*Sollicitudo Rei Socialis*, nos. 9-10). The commitment to the development of peoples is both an individual and a collective obligation (no. 32) and development should be based on fundamental equality of persons and peoples (no. 33).

John Paul II differs, however, in his prescriptions by emphasizing personalist solutions over institutional ones. This shift can be seen in two ways. First, in *Sollicitudo Rei Socialis*, solidarity is a learned disposition, which propels one person or groups of people to identify with, stand by, and take upon themselves the burden of the poor. In taking their burdens on, those practicing solidarity seek to assist the poor, those whose capabilities are limited by the accidents of their birth, location, or human wickedness. According to *Sollicitudo Rei Socialis*, solidarity is both a virtue and a principle (no. 38). Hence, Christians who do not exhibit solidarity are unchristian because that failure goes against an "essential Christian ethic."[11]

For Paul VI in *Populorum Progressio*, solidarity leans more toward justice than personal virtue. To realize equity in the world, Paul VI envisions a justice outlook that should raise taxes for the rich (nos. 47, 84) in order that "public authorities may expand their efforts in the work of development" (no. 47). This implies a primary role for government, because voluntarist approaches and intermediary initiatives are insufficient to redress global inequity today (no. 33). Nevertheless, this significant role for government must not stifle human liberty and other fundamental human rights (no. 33). Accordingly, Paul VI proposes that public and international institutions should seek to redress the political and economic imbalances of colonialism, neo-colonialism, the ideology-driven Cold War, globalization (nos. 33, 78), and "economic dictatorship" (no. 59). Fair trade agreements based on equality of partnership and opportunity are crucial for *Populorum Progressio*'s view of authentic development, to counter double standards in trade deals among nations (no. 61).

Second, *Populorum Progressio* and *Sollicitudo Rei Socialis* differ in their emphasis on the preferential option for the poor. Even though *Populorum Progressio* does not use the phrase, the idea is expressed through the document's critiques of "'unjust structures'" and "social patterns that can be called forms of 'institutionalized violence'."[12] Hence, *Populorum Progressio* emphasizes that, without tangible restoration of human dignity and return of what was forcefully taken (during imperial and colonial periods) or what was expropriated through unfair trade deals (through neoliberalism or globalization), there cannot be just peace and harmony. This is why *Populorum Progressio* emphasizes justice and institutional responses to unjust structures, including those that limit people's capabilities (e.g. nos. 77, 78, 84).

In *Sollicitudo Rei Socialis*, John Paul II leans more toward love, emphasizing voluntarism and subordinating justice. Instead of the "preferential option for the poor," *Sollicitudo Rei Socialis* contains a nuanced rephrasing of it: "the option or love of preference for the

---

[11] For this term, see Richard McCormick, "Theology and Bioethics," *Hastings Center Report* 19, no. 2 (March/April 1989): 6-7. For him, an "essential Christian ethic" refers to ethical decisions a Christian must make precisely because one is a Christian. These decisions are non-binding on a non-Christian.

[12] David Hollenbach, "Commentary on *Gaudium et spes* (*Pastoral Constitution on the Church in the Modern World*)," in *Modern Catholic Social Teaching: Commentaries and Interpretations*, ed. Kenneth R. Himes, O.F.M. (Washington, DC: Georgetown University Press, 2005), 287.

poor" (no. 42). Implicitly in *Populorum Progressio*, and quite explicitly in the 1971 Synod of Bishops document *Justice in the World*, the
option for the poor is understood within the context of the "duties of
justice" (no. 30) and "God's absolute demand for justice and love"
(no. 34). Like *Populorum Progressio*, *Sollicitudo Rei Socialis* wishes
to affirm the importance of demonstrating concern for the poor and
their fate. However, since the phrase "option for the poor" appears to
be central to the radicalism of liberation theology and its problematic
association with Marxist ideology, John Paul II rephrases "preferential
option for the poor" to "love of preference for the poor" (no. 42) in
order to distance his ideas from the liberation theology movement.[13]

Thus, *Sollicitudo Rei Socialis* moves to a more personalist response
to the social problem, shifting away from *Populorum Progressio*'s institutional emphasis. John Paul II's understanding of "solidarity" as
the prescription for the social question echoes more of love with its
supererogatory and self-sacrificing nature (nos. 38, 40). Solidarity is
reckoned as a specifically Christian virtue, characterized by gratuitousness (no. 40). "Structures of sin" and "evil mechanisms" at work
within nations and within the international order can be overcome only
through the logic of the gratuitousness of solidarity (*Sollicitudo Rei
Socialis*, no. 40). *Sollicitudo Rei Socialis'* examples of solidarity from
the Christian Tradition include canonized saints like "St. Peter Claver
and his service to the slaves at Cartagena de Indias, and St. Maximilian
Maria Kolbe who offered his life in place of a prisoner unknown to
him in the concentration camp at Auschwitz" (no. 40).

Populorum Progressio maintains a firm connection between solidarity and justice, echoing Pius XII's motto, "*Opus iustitiae pax.*" *Sollicitudo Rei Socialis* replaces *opus iustititae pax* with *opus solidarita-
tis pax* (no. 39). While Paul VI strongly affirms that "If you want
peace, work for justice", as in his 1972 World Day of Peace Message,[14] John Paul II indicates that it is solidarity (social love) that can
bring peace. Although John Paul II refers to solidarity as a principle,
value, virtue, and duty (nos. 38, 40), "it seems both from his understanding in *Sollicitudo rei socialis* and from the understanding of
moral theory in general that primacy should be given to solidarity as a

---

[13] Here we see an instance of co-optation of the language of liberation theology by
its avowed critics in order to give the impression that they are not against certain
ideas of the movement. Co-optation is a strategy of dulling the radicalism of the liberation theology movement and making it compatible with capitalist ideology. See
Ivan Peterella, *The Future of Liberation Theology: An Argument and Manifesto*
(Vermont: Ashgate, 2004), for this idea.
[14] Paul VI acknowledges that this is based on Isaiah 32:17: "Justice will bring about
Peace." See Paul VI, "Message for the Celebration of the Day of Peace - 1 January
1972," www.vatican.va/holy_father/paul_vi/messages/peace/ documents/hf_p-
vi_mes_19711208_v-world-day-for-peace_en.html.

virtue."[15] This emphasis laid *Sollicitudo Rei Socialis* open to stringent criticisms that it placed too much thrust on individual choices while it departs from "mainstream Catholic social teaching" because it ignores "structural criticisms concerning the causes of poverty, and by disregarding radical prescriptions of what might be done about poverty."[16]

Though one can say solidarity is a virtue, in *Populorum Progressio* it is firmly an ethical imperative. Moreover, it is not just for the Christian, a contrast with *Sollicitudo Rei Socialis* which avers that solidarity is a Christian value. Perhaps in seeking to offer a Christological foundation for human responses to the social question, *Sollicitudo Rei Socialis* may have limited attraction for women and men of goodwill who might find *Populorum Progressio* more suitable as a dialogue partner in a pluralist society. Maybe this is why fifty years after its drafting, *Populorum Progressio* still resonates in the church and the world.

While *Centesimus Annus* does not articulate the core issues of *Populorum Progressio*, it does continue *Sollicitudo Rei Socialis'* move of solidarity away from an action of justice and structural change and toward a virtue and principle fostering personal change. *Centesimus Annus* primarily reflects on *Rerum Novarum's* social question in the light of the events of 1989. Consequently, *Centesimus Annus'* third chapter is titled "The Year 1989." The contemporary social question centers on labor, work, and workers. International economic restructuring and globalization in the light of the collapse of the Soviet Union and Communism and the apparent victory of Western-styled capitalist economic model are *Centesimus Annus'* main concern. Human dignity, non-violent resistance, free but fair market economies, the common good, limited states, and states' welfare services form John Paul II's reflection on a post-1989 world, especially Eastern Europe.

As the former Eastern bloc adopted the only surviving economic ideology, *Centesimus Annus* offers some exhortation and guidelines. Unbridled capitalism that disregards persons, especially workers, is still with us. *Centesimus Annus'* third chapter rejects triumphalism that proclaims capitalism now as "the only model of economic organization" after the defeat of socialism (no. 35). Capitalism still has inbuilt injustice like monopolies and barriers against authentic development. A new form of capitalism is not about material acquisition but the financialization of wealth. Yet, in chapter four, John Paul II writes

---

[15] Charles E. Curran, Kenneth R, Himes, O.F.M., and Thomas E. Shannon, "Commentary on *Sollicitudo rei socialis (On Social Concern),*" in *Modern Catholic Social Teaching: Commentaries and Interpretations,* ed. Kenneth R. Himes, O.F.M. (Washington, DC: Georgetown University Press, 2005), 430.

[16] Curran, Himes, and Shannon, "Commentary on *Sollicitudo rei socialis,*" 432-33.

that capitalism as a "free economy" and "pro-business" is "the victorious social system" and "the goal for countries now making efforts to rebuild their economy and society" (no. 42).

Thus, *Centesimus Annus* favors an approach to global equality and justice that emphasizes free enterprise and the increased capability of citizens. The state is given a limited role because of a noticeable aversion toward the welfare state. This is why one might say *Centesimus Annus* contains an endorsement of capitalism, at least in chapter five.[17] Capitalism is perceived as the only economic model that can protect the individual from the intrusion and danger inherent in the welfare state. Hence, calls for collective actions made in *Centesimus Annus* should be seen from the fundamental perspective of the limited role and distrust of a state with increased power. Institutional responses to injustice mean institutions of private citizens bound together by a common sense of solidarity.

POPE BENEDICT XVI'S PERSPECTIVE

Although justice is not extraneous to charity, Benedict XVI's *Caritas in Veritate* continues the trend in recent magisterial teachings to subordinate justice to love by his claim that justice is a practical form of charity.[18] This trend continues in the choice of the common good as the second practical form of charity, instead of the more traditional universal destination of goods. The common good, in *Caritas in Veritate*, is rooted in the idea that to love is to desire the good of the recipient of love and to ensure that the good is secured (no. 7). The good that links all persons joined together in a society is understood as the common good. Hence, in everyone's circumstance and situation the ethical obligation is to strive for that common good.

Caritas in Veritate takes the voluntariness of those obliged to the common good for granted. Verstraeten shows that this voluntariness is characteristic of official church teaching's gradual buying into the

---

[17] I agree with Johan Verstraeten that the fourth chapter of the encyclical contains numerous nuances about capitalism such that one cannot say unequivocally that *Centesimus Annus* uncritically accepts capitalism. However, the stringent criticisms against the welfare state in chapter five echo the criticisms of the liberal and anti-liberationist lobby, especially in North America, exemplified by Michael Novak, who is regarded by some as one of *Centesimus Annus'* "ghost writers." See Johan Verstraeten, "Justice Subordinated to Love?: The Changing Agenda of Catholic Social Teaching since *Populorum Progressio*," in *Responsibility, God and Society: Theological Ethics in Dialogue*, ed. Johan De Tavernier (Leuven: Peeters, 2008), 394-400.

[18] In chapter one, *Caritas in Veritate* states that justice, peace and development are expressions of divine gratuitousness (no. 15). This is quite different from Vatican II's *Gaudium et Spes* where the overarching principles for a just world are justice and universal destination of goods. Peace, from this perspective, is "an enterprise of justice." It follows or flows from justice (*Gaudium et Spes*, nos. 66, 69, 77).

logic of the free market – as a safeguard against Marxist-tainted alternative economies.[19] This is not accidental because *Caritas in Veritate*'s discussion on justice, solidarity, and responsibility is found largely in the third chapter titled "Fraternity, Economic Development and Civil Society." The whole discussion on justice is subsumed within the overarching principle of gratuitousness and friendship.

Despite *Caritas in Veritate*'s nuanced critical stance against neoliberal economics, it still remains the *de facto* model. The economic meltdown of 2007-2008 is not sufficient to search for an alternative model. The meltdown arose due to the malfunctioning and "dramatic problems" of a system that has supposedly brought about amazing economic growth (no. 21). So, the solution lies in a cultural renewal and rediscovery of "fundamental values on which to build a better future" (no. 21). Later, we read that what is needed is "a profound and far-sighted revision of the current model of development, so as to correct its dysfunctions and deviations" (no. 32).

Africae Munus is the post-synodal exhortation issued after the Second Special Assembly of Bishops for Africa. Following the teachings of *Caritas in Veritate, Africae Munus* avers that authentic development, especially in societies emerging from violent conflicts or repressive dictatorship, needs the principles of subsidiarity and solidarity to sustain the practice of justice. Subsidiarity ensures that for justice to flourish the higher authority must not usurp the sovereignty and competence of lower but competent authorities (no. 24). Solidarity ensures that excesses in wealth and resources are shared with the poor. Balancing the demands of subsidiarity and solidarity requires justice. However, justice must be inspired by the virtue of *caritas*, must be inspired by love's logic of superabundance (nos. 26-28). Together with *Caritas in Veritate, Africae Munus* follows the trajectory begun by John Paul II of moving away from structural change and institutional actions and toward an emphasis on social endeavors and personal actions. It is a shift away from understanding solidarity as a work of justice obliging everyone to a principle only binding individual Christians.

THE PROBLEMATIC SPLIT BETWEEN 'CARITAS' AND 'IUSTITIA'

The split between charity and justice as demonstrated in the post-Paul VI pontificates makes sense within stable Western democracies that are the products of Western modernity. The articulation of ecclesial mission and its ethical responsibility during modernity was largely Western, middle class, and clerical. It was informed by modernity's "separation of church and state." Hence, charity, more like humanitarian assistance clothed in an evangelical cloak, came to characterize the ecclesial mission. Justice was for the state.

---

[19] See Verstraeten, "Justice Subordinated to Love?," 393, 394, 397-399.

Splitting justice and charity, however, meant that systemic problems were rarely addressed and assistance provided aid (in theory) but
not the needed change. Out of several regions in the world, I have sin-
gled out Sub-Saharan Africa because this sub-region is my immediate
context. Africa is the second largest continent in the world, with the
largest growing population. It is a resource rich continent coveted by
all.[20] Paradoxically, this continent appears irrelevant in the twenty-
first century. Though its resources are endlessly extracted and shipped
to the West for processing, it contributes just "one percent of international trade, barely enough diplomatic influence to match its small
economic role, and modest military forces trained only on itself."[21]
Apart from their exotic dressing and loud music, Africans are scarcely
noticed.[22] Nonetheless, Africa contributes a staggering amount to the
wealth of the wealthiest one percent. According to an Oxfam report,
An Economy for the 1%, released on the eve of the 2016 World Economic Forum,

> Almost a third (30%) of rich Africans' wealth – a total of $500bn – is
> held offshore in tax havens. It is estimated that this costs African coun-
> tries $14bn a year in lost tax revenues. This is enough money to pay
> for healthcare that could save the lives of 4 million children and em-
> ploy enough teachers to get every African child into school.[23]

This tragic paradox pricks the conscience of some who want to end
such glaring poverty. They engage in projects and advocacies to lift
the 'bottom billion' out of poverty.[24] Paramount to their development
model, though, is social-economic growth along indices informed by
the neo-liberal economic model.[25]

Indeed, this development model is markedly different from *Populorum Progressio*'s holistic development. *Populorum Progressio* is
concerned about development such that we are not allowed to do what
is morally obnoxious to bring about good (nos. 30-31). It calls for justice, for individuals of all perspectives to address the wrongs. Conversely, development do-gooders focus on more individual aid than
structural change, charity over justice. In order to get potential donors

---

[20] Raymond Olusesan Aina, "Images of Africa and the Resilience of Ignorance,"
Zeitschrift für internationale Bildungsforschungund Entwicklungspädagogik 37, no.
4 (2014): 26.
[21] Robert Calderisi, *The Trouble with Africa: Why Foreign Aid Isn't Working* (Connecticut: Yale University Press, 2006), 4.
[22] Thandika Mkandawire, "Running While Others Walk: Knowledge and the Challenge of Africa's Development," *Africa Development* 36, no. 2 (2011): 2.
[23] Hardoon, Ayele and Fuentes-Nieva, *An Economy for the 1%*, 5.
[24] Paul Collier, *The Bottom Billion: Why the Poorest Countries Are Failing and
What Can Be Done About It* (New York: Oxford University Press, 2008), 4, 100.
[25] Rama Mani, *Beyond Retribution: Seeking Justice in the Shadows of War* (Cambridge: Polity, 2002), 126-147.

to give maximally, "development pornography" blossomed. "Development pornography" or *poornography* means showing off the poor's nudity as part of the strategy to raise monies in the West. This is done without consideration of its ethical propriety.[26] According to Quist-Adade and van Wyk, *poornography* becomes a tool "to gain maximum donor response." *Poornography* is "'compassion usury' ... to mobilize the public's conscience and support."[27] The problem with the development "business" is that it is carried out by aid agencies that get contracts for their projects anywhere in the world except the real bottom (Chad, Laos, Central African Republic, Niger).[28] So, though poverty gets attention, it is based on simplistic moralization, or what Paul Collier calls "a headless heart."[29] In spite of these efforts, the obscene gap between the rich and the poor is increasing. In addition to the ineffectiveness of this aid, systemic corruption affects governments in Africa.[30] Robert Calderisi is correct in saying, "Corruption is endemic in Africa for the same reasons as elsewhere. But it hurts the continent more than other regions, is more brazen, and accepted more readily. As much of the elite is involved, and the poor are powerless, there is little pressure for change."[31] This is not peculiar to Africa. According to Pope Francis's *Evangelii Gaudium*, there is "widespread and deeply rooted corruption found in many countries – in their governments, businesses and institutions – whatever the political ideology of their leaders" (no. 60).

Sometimes, peoples of the South sense that the hackneyed call for reforms is good news even to the major actors in the West, where most of the policies of misery originate and where the immorally expropriated wealth is stashed. For instance, the International Monetary Fund, World Bank, and Western governments are contributing to the Democratic Republic of Congo (DRC) disaster while these same institutions are '"rewarding" Rwanda and Uganda for their crimes against

---

[26] Charles Quist-Adade and Anita van Wyk, "The Role of NGOs in Canada and the USA in the Transformation of the Socio-Cultural Structures in Africa," *Africa Development* 32, no. 2 (2007): 81.

[27] Quist-Adade and van Wyk, "The Role of NGOs," 81.

[28] Collier, *The Bottom Billion*, 4. Not all development experts have ulterior motives and utilitarian considerations, but altruistic development experts are few and far between. See Aina, "Images of Africa," 26-27.

[29] Collier, *The Bottom Billion*, 4.

[30] "Chop Fine: The Human Rights Impact of Local Government Corruption and Mismanagement in Rivers State, Nigeria," *Human Rights Watch* 19, no. 2A (January 2007): 17-18; Christine Wanjiru Gichure, *Ethics for Africa Today: An Introduction to Business Ethics* (Nairobi: Paulines Publication Africa, 2008), 150-162.

[31] Calderisi, *Trouble with Africa*, 90.

humanity in the DRC because the gold and diamond they illegally extract from the DRC find their way to Western Europe.[32] According to Raymond Banker, a former World Bank executive, all corrupt monies coming from these developed countries are about $500 billion per year. Annually, $50 billion comes as development aid from the West to poor countries, while $500 billion in "dirty money" are freighted offshore and stashed in offshore accounts in developed and highly industrialized nations. These monies are tax-free.[33] The Oxfam report released in January 2016 shortly before the annual World Economic Forum and the Panama Papers[34] scandal poignantly confirm assertions like Baker's.[35]

In the face of these issues, being a crucial member of civil society in many countries of the South, ravaged by the effects of colonialism and post-colonialism, the church's ecclesial mission cannot regard justice as merely instrumental to the Church's mission, as implied by the works of John Paul II and Benedict XVI noted above. In some places in the South, the church can be the only viable institution that can promote – even pursue – justice for the people. Some years ago, the Catholic bishops in southern Nigeria formed a body called the "Niger Delta Catholic Bishops Forum" under the aegis of the Catholic Bishops' Conference of Nigeria. These bishops are overseeing the Catholic Church in the volatile Niger Delta region that has suffered deprivation and environmental degradation due to the oil exploration of unscrupulous oil companies. After years of exhortation and proclamation, I see this forum as an uncommon attempt (at least in Sub-Saharan Africa) to break the boundary – or rather close the gap – between charity and justice and so harken back to Paul VI's *Populorum Progressio*.

POPULORUM PROGRESSIO AND SUB-SAHARAN AFRICA: INSPIRATION AND RELEVANCE

One can safely aver that *Populorum Progressio* is concerned about those left behind, who are not enjoying globalization's benefits. It is more of a concern to let the "other" be seen as a neighbor to whom one has responsibility beyond the limitations of the modern state. In a world where the gap is widening between the rich and the poor, especially between the Global North and South, the humanism that is the foundation of the existing economic order and international structures

---

[32] Timothy Reid, "Killing Them Softly: Has Foreign Aid to Rwanda and Uganda Contributed to the Humanitarian Tragedy in the DRC?," *Africa Policy Journal* 1 (Spring 2006): 74-94.

[33] Raymond Baker, *Capitalism's Achilles Heel: Dirty Money and How to Renew the Free-Market System* (Hoboken: Wiley, 2005), 248.

[34] The Panama Papers are the confidential papers from Fonseca, a legal firm in Panama, which reveal how several individuals and organizations falsely register phony companies in various tax havens just to evade taxes.

[35] Hardoon, Ayele and Fuentes-Nieva, *An Economy for the 1%*, 19-26.

is not human enough. In the light of prevailing conditions in Africa that mirror *Populorum Progressio's* analysis, what can one say about the way forward?

The powers in the West and the developing countries will keep listening condescendingly to those moral authorities appealing to them to reform, as long as no one asks for or gives moral support to radical system change or revolution that can threaten their interests. Perhaps this fact reveals a limitation of Catholic Social Teaching to peoples of the South regardless of the hope the teaching offers. Official Catholic Social Teaching's accent is on harmony and consensus. This approach believes that confrontation and some degree of conflict are incompatible with the pursuit of social justice. On the contrary, emphasis is on agreement and cooperation with all who desire a better world.[36] It appears that the church's commitment to social justice will best be realized by emphasizing a social doctrine that seeks to pursue the stability of the society and concord among various segments of the society.[37] The church does not wish to be seen as inciting the poor and emasculated from laying claims to their just entitlement.

However, there may be times the church has to move from preference for harmony and consensus to confrontation and partisanship for the sake of social justice. This is reasonable if the Body of Christ remains true to its practical hope in the promise that Christ has come to bring abundant life. Therein lies the tension between the hierarchy and liberation theologians. Liberation theologians contend that "liberation" of the poor should replace "development." The former emphasizes the poor becoming subjects of their destiny and liberation, and the latter replicates "Western thought-patterns and values," is spearheaded by Western-dominated nations and institutions, and covers up practices that exploit poor countries and their long-suffering peoples.[38] This is where one sees another inspiration from *Populorum Progressio* in addition to the call for structural change. In my opinion,

---

[36] Lisa Cahill, "Practical Hope: Today's Challenge," in *Scrutinizing the Signs of the Times in the Light of the Gospel*, ed. Johan Verstraeten (Leuven: University Press, 2007), 312.

[37] Donal Dorr, "The Perspective of the Poor: What We Can Learn from Liberation Theology about the 'Signs of the Times'," in *Scrutinizing the Signs of the Times in the Light of the Gospel*, ed. Johan Verstraeten (Leuven: University Press, 2007), 264-266.

[38] Dorr, "The Perspective of the Poor," 268-69. Unlike Dorr, non-religious development studies experts do not dispense with the word "development." However, authentic development, especially in the South, is resistance. This means, in the words of Yash Tandon, "the satisfaction of the basic material and social needs of the people (especially those most vulnerable) through a system of governance that is democratic and accountable to the people, and through eliminating imperial interventions in developing societies." This notion of development attends to contextual realities and therefore rejects the one-size-fits-all of pro-establishment experts. See Yash Tandon, "Development is Resistance," *Africa Development* 40, no. 3 (2015): 147.

"revolution" in *Populorum Progressio* is a mass mobilization against real or perceived unjust political structure and authority. This mobilization can lead to violent regime change, or grave undermining of hitherto legitimate authority that oppressed human reason and freedom. As used in *Populorum Progressio*, revolution cannot be incremental. It is massive, chaotic, and aggressively antinomian (and in many cases anti-religion). Hence, it appears revolution is necessarily violent and hence incompatible with Christian pacifism.

Yet, revolution does not necessarily have to be violent and disorderly. Any organized movement of the people that seeks to structurally transform the social environment that had inhibited freedom and capability is revolutionary in that broad sense. This movement is not merely about reform. It is about the pursuit of a fresh historical project that seeks to liberate the poor and marginalized from the structures of sin which are inhibiting their capabilities and flourishing. This pursuit hinges on a conviction that another world is possible.

Thus, the church in the South considers it as part of its contextually sensitive ecclesial mission to provoke and advocate for viable "alternative forms of market economies."[39] A proactive ecclesial mission for justice and human flourishing has a responsibility ethic, which argues that socio-economic and distributive justice for people cannot be based on utilitarianism, or pragmatism, or consequentialism. On the contrary, a proactive church in the South inspired by *Populorum Progressio* affirms that a responsibility ethic may just be what economic systems and policies in the South need. This ethic can be concretized in public fora for creative but marginalized visionary economists and experts who are offering alternative forms of market economies like those in Sweden, or the European social democratic model.

Contrary to the Anglo-American market model, which has made countries in the South whittle away some of their socialist structural legacies, the European (especially the Scandinavian countries) social model needs to be presented to the African public for consideration. This alternative social model is characterized by a "sustained robust growth ... marked with better health care and education ...."[40] It has strategic protective barriers, subsidies for exports and "nationalized or highly concentrated, private industry"[41] until the countries are competitive in the global market, as done by Japan, Singapore and Malaysia. Western Europe did this after World War II, and the United States did this during the Great Depression of the 1930s. It gave rise to the famed New Deal and its Keynesian revolution which "provided the rationale for a more active, interventionist state in the regulation of

---

[39] Joseph Stiglitz, *Making Globalization Work* (New York: Norton, 2006), 9.
[40] Stiglitz, *Making Globalization Work*, xv.
[41] Stiglitz, *Making Globalization Work*, xv.

economic activity with the capitalist economy."[42] When there are no fora for visionary revolutionaries of the South to put forward alternative economic models, peoples of the South cannot insist on the kind of economic and fiscal systems they want. Hence, decision-making remains with the technocrats, trained in market fundamentalism, who are equally more insulated from the obscene inequality in rural areas and the growing slums around the megacities.

CONCLUSION

Populorum Progressio offers firm Christian hope that another world beyond inequality is possible. Hope is decisive for humans who live in a liminal state (i.e. a life of "in-between") characterized by, on the one hand, an orientation towards fulfilment and, on the other hand, an awareness that this future will not be fully achieved in the here and now. Reflecting on this encyclical fifty years after its publication, I appreciate the fact that humans are pilgrims who are constantly on the way yet persistently challenged to be confident that "ultimate blessedness will not be betrayed."[43] The *Compendium of the Social Doctrine of the Church* is right in one of its concluding paragraphs: "Christian hope lends great energy to commitment in the social field, because it generates confidence in the possibility of building a better world, even if there will never exist 'a paradise of earth'" (no. 570). Accordingly, even if outside the Roman Catholic Church today *Populorum Progressio* apparently sounds like a distant echo in an obscenely unequal world, the hope this encyclical offers still endures. The decisive interventions of Pope Francis' pontificate so far gives the confidence that perhaps the radical vision of *Populorum Progressio* and other church documents of the sixties and seventies on the social question might be experiencing a new spring time. This undoubtedly gladdens the People of God in the South. ⧄

---

[42] John Foster, "Contradictions in the Universalization of Capitalism," *Monthly Review* 50, no. 1 (April 1999): 33.
[43] Paul Wadell, "Hope," in *The Collegeville Pastoral Dictionary of Biblical Theology*, ed. Carroll Stuhlmueller (Minnesota: Liturgical Press, 1996), 438.

Journal of Moral Theology, Vol. 6, No. 1 (2017): 112-129

Pacis Progressio: How Francis' Four New Principles Develop Catholic Social Teaching into Catholic Social Praxis

Barrett Turner

> In the end, a peace which is not the result of integral development will be doomed.
> —Francis, *Evangelii Gaudium*, no. 219

N ASSESSING THE DYNAMICS of the Catholic Church's social doctrine, Russell Hittinger has noted that the "tradition is not only multi-disciplinary, but internally multi-faceted as one pope introduces new themes even while circling back upon the work of his predecessors. It is the Roman way to introduce new considerations while at the same time tightening their connection to the preceding tradition."[1] Pope Francis has tightened the connection of his magisterium to that of prior popes in relying on Paul VI for the link between evangelization and development in *Evangelii Gaudium* and in recapitulating and expanding upon the teaching of John Paul II and Benedict XVI on care for creation in *Laudato Si'*. Yet what are the "new considerations" in Francis' contribution to Catholic social doctrine? One is his proposal of four new principles of Catholic social teaching in *Evangelii Gaudium*, nos. 217-237, principles that complete the work of Paul VI on evangelization and development: time is greater than space, realities are greater than ideas, unity prevails over conflict, and the whole is greater than the part. These four principles are a uniquely Latin American contribution—born of the Latin and South American struggles to achieve the common good amidst the residue of colonialism, economic ideologies, violence, and poverty—and, while drawing on the classic principles of Catholic social teaching, return to the mode of praxis. One might best think of them as maxims for practicing Catholic social teaching, maxims themselves normed by the theoretical content of what the common good is but adding the element of how to achieve it.

---

[1] Russell Hittinger, "The Coherence of the Four Basic Principles of Catholic Social Doctrine: An Interpretation," in *Pursuing the Common Good: How Solidarity and Subsidiarity Can Work Together*, ed. Margaret S. Archer and Pierpaolo Donati (Vatican City: Pontifical Academy of Social Sciences, 2008), 77. On the "Roman way," see Rémi Brague, *Europe, la voie romaine* (Paris: Éditions Critérion, 1992), which argues that the essential cultural mode of Europe is the Roman capability of recognizing and assimilating superior sources of culture outside of itself in a constant process of renewal.

This paper will first outline the history and prevalence of the new principles in the magisterium of Francis. He used these principles prior to becoming pope in response to the growing Catholic emphasis in the 1970s on the pursuit of social justice as integral to faith. In many ways, the key link between faith and justice was made in Paul VI's *Populorum Progressio* and *Evangelii Nuntiandi*. Since becoming pope, Francis has referred frequently to these new principles in both written and oral settings. Second, the paper will explain the nature of Francis' new principles within their setting in *Evangelii Gaudium* and why Francis holds that these principles emerge from the nature of society itself on the one hand and from the tenets of Catholic social teaching on the other. This section will therefore expand upon Francis' remarks by using Juan Carlos Scannone's recent suggestion that, in these principles, Francis is indebted to the thought of Romano Guardini, albeit in application to Latin American ecclesial and social questions.[2] Third, the paper will explain how Francis understands Catholic social teaching as a praxis, a necessary means to the end of social peace through participation and dialogue. For Francis, Catholic social teaching is a praxis that anticipates and even constitutes social peace.

ORIGINS OF THE NEW "BERGOLIAN" PRINCIPLES

As pointed out by Scannone, Francis has been thinking with these new principles since his 1974 talk as provincial of the Jesuit Argentinian province.[3] While not denying the uniquely Argentinian and personal sources of Francis' principles, one should observe that Francis articulates his principles in a period in which the Church was discerning the relationship between evangelization and social development. Paul VI's 1967 encyclical *Populorum Progressio* held out the concept of integral human development, which is "the development of each man and the whole man" (no. 15), a "true humanism" that is "open to values of the spirit and to God who is their source" (no. 42). Integral human development entails that the human person's material, economic, social, and spiritual needs should ultimately not be separated, not only in theory but even in practice, and must be pursued in society simultaneously. The historical context for Paul's insistence on the "integral" nature of human development included the inability of the United Nations to issue a unified rights treaty in 1966, instead issuing two separate covenants, one on civil and political rights and one on economic, social, and cultural rights.[4] Western nations in particular

---

[2] Juan Carlos Scannone, SJ, "Pope Francis and the Theology of the People," *Theological Studies* 77, no. 1 (2016): 118-135, 129.

[3] Scannone, "Pope Francis and the Theology of the People," 128, note 32; See also, Austen Ivereigh, *The Great Reformer: Francis and the Making of a Radical Pope, Second Edition* (New York: Picador, 2015), 140-43.

[4] United Nations, "International Covenant on Civil and Political Rights (December 16th, 1966)," *United Nations Treaty Series* 999 (1976): 171-301; United Nations,

hesitated to pursue a unified document, since they denied an equivalent urgency and force to economic and social rights as they did to
civil rights, belying official UN rhetoric about the unicity of all human
rights.[5] To the contrary, Paul noted that "political freedom is not
enough" and that nations "must also acquire the social and economic
structures and processes that accord with man's nature and activity"
(no. 6). On the Church's role in development, Paul also noted, "True
to the teaching and example of her divine Founder, who cited the
preaching of the Gospel to the poor as a sign of his mission, the Church
has never failed to foster the human progress of the nations to which
she brings the faith in Christ" (no. 12). This connection of the
Church's activity in evangelization to integral human development,
even if presented in a somewhat accidental manner, inspired continued
conversation about how the Gospel and social justice cohere. In this
way, *Populorum Progressio* continued the papal magisterial concern
for ensuring participation, now directed against a neocolonialism in
which poorer, less developed states were hindered from participation
at the international level on account of foreign political and economic
pressure.[6]

   In the wake of Paul's intervention, both regional and universal
gatherings of bishops responded by more explicitly linking together
the spiritual good of the person (to which the gospel pertains) and the
material and social good of the person (to which Catholic social teaching speaks). The Episcopal Conference of Latin American and the
Caribbean (CELAM) issued a comprehensive document at Medellín
in 1968 that included discussions of justice, peace, social structures,
catechesis, and the poverty of the Church.[7] In 1971, the second Synod
of Bishops issued "Justice in the World," in which the bishops claimed
at the end of their introduction that "action for justice and participation
in the transformation of the world appear clearly to us as a constitutive
dimension of the preaching of the Gospel, that is to say, of the
Church's mission in favor of the human race's redemption and liberation from all oppressive situations."[8] The Synod of Bishops returned

---

"International Covenant on Economic, Social and Cultural Rights (December 16th,
1966)," *United Nations Treaty Series* 993 (1976): 3-106.
[5] Sarah Joseph and Melissa Castan, *The International Covenant on Civil and Political Rights: Cases, Materials, and Commentary, Third Edition* (Oxford: Oxford University Press, 2013), 7.
[6] Michael J. Schuck, *That They Be One: The Social Teaching of Papal Encyclicals
1740-1989* (Washington, DC: Georgetown University Press, 1991), 120-21; See
also, Allan Figueroa Deck, SJ, "Commentary on *Populorum progressio*," in *Modern
Catholic Social Teaching: Commentaries and Interpretations*, ed. Kenneth R. Himes
(Washington, DC: Georgetown University Press, 2005), 292.
[7] CELAM, "Documentos finales de Medellín," www.celam.org/conferencia_medel-
lin.php.
[8] Synod of Bishops, "A justiça no mundo," www.vatican.va/roman_curia/synod/doc-
uments /rc_synod_doc_19711130_giustizia_po.html.

to this question of evangelization and justice in their third meeting in 1974, "Evangelization in the Modern World," to which Paul VI responded with his 1974 post-synodal exhortation *Evangelii Nuntiandi*. While focused on the proclamation of the gospel as essential to the Church's activity, Paul also noted that:

> Evangelization would not be complete if it did not take account of the unceasing interplay of the Gospel and of man's concrete life, both personal and social. This is why evangelization involves an explicit message ... about the rights and duties of every human being, about family life ..., about life in society, about international life, peace, justice and development—a message especially energetic today about liberation. (no. 29)

Shortly thereafter, the Society of Jesus modified their mission under the leadership of superior general Pedro Arrupe at General Congregation 32 in late 1974 and early 1975. Appealing to both the 1971 and 1974 synods, Decree Four claimed that the current world situation demanded that the Jesuits reinterpret their mission in light of the fact that "the promotion of justice is an absolute requirement" in "the service of faith."[9]

The connection between the Argentinian "Theology of the People" and Catholic social teaching was established in this period of interplay between papal and regional episcopal teaching documents.[10] It is well known that the work of Argentines Fr. Lucio Gera, the founder of *teología del pueblo*, and Eduardo Cardinal Pironio, present at the 1974 synod, influenced Paul VI's *Evangelii Nuntiandi*, especially in Paul's emphasis on the evangelization of culture (e.g., no. 20). This Argentine strand of liberation theology included the emphasis on the liberation of the poor common to other liberation theologies, doing so not on the Marxist economic or political concerns animating other strands

---

[9] Society of Jesus, General Congregation 32, Decree 4, no. 2 (1975). See also Ivereigh, *The Great Reformer*, 120-121. Ivereigh quotes a Fr. Swinnen as saying that Bergoglio "did not have much sympathy for that Decree Four" and never quoted the document when forming Jesuit novices (121). Recently, however, Francis cited Decree Four in his discourse to General Congregation 36 of the Society of Jesus (gc36.org/wp-content/uploads/2016/10/20161024_Discourse_Pope_GC36_EN.pdf): "The Lord who looks at us with mercy and chooses us, sends us out to bring with all its effectiveness, that same mercy to the poorest, to sinners, to those discarded people, and those crucified in the present world, who suffer injustice and violence. Only if we experience the healing power first-hand in our own wounds, as people and as a body, will we lose the fear of allowing ourselves to be moved by the immense suffering of our brothers and sisters, and will we hasten to walk patiently with our people, learning from them the best way of helping and serving them. (cf. General Congregation 32, d. 4 n. 50)"

[10] This paragraph closely follows the histories of Scannone, "Pope Francis and the Theology of the People," 120, 123-124, and Ivereigh, *The Great Reformer*, 184-185.

but through a focus on the history and culture of the people. The 1979 CELAM meeting in Puebla yielded another document that drew upon *Evangelii Nuntiandi* in order to deepen Latin American discussions of the place of culture and popular religiosity in evangelization.[11] The Argentinian version of liberation theology thus answered the question of how evangelization and social justice are linked by reference to the life of "God's faithful people." In addition, Bergoglio's particular struggles with political parties, economic ideologies, and abuses of state power in Argentina confirmed for him this focus on the people as the subject of development. From the divisions suffered by the people along Marxist and Peronist lines in the "dirty war" of the 1970s up to the corruption of the Kirchners in the 2000s, Bergoglio would constantly keep his focus on what was necessary to serve the people, who were living at the peripheries of the elites' ideological programs. He therefore developed his four principles in relation to constant tensions in Argentine social questions, tensions that were being reduced, collapsed, or ignored by the predominant powers. It is for this reason that Ivereigh calls Bergoglio's four principles "anti-ideological" and working against "the schemes of the elites."[12]

One should therefore understand Francis' four new principles as originating from, entering into, and completing this period's debate about the essential link between evangelization and social justice by proposing and developing an Argentine way of reconciling faith and justice in the task of "building a people." Like Paul's *Evangelii Nuntiandi*, Francis' exhortation responds to a meeting of the Synod of Bishops about evangelization, this time the 2012 synod on "New Evangelization and the Transmission of the Christian Faith." Francis gives his fullest magisterial description of the four principles in the post-synodal apostolic exhortation *Evangelii Gaudium*, proposing for the universal Church his principles worked out in conversation with the "theology of the people." In the context of the social dimension of Christian evangelization, Francis addresses "building a people" in justice and peace together with Christian discipleship. It therefore should also not surprise anyone that Francis draws from *Populorum Progressio* and *Evangelii Nuntiandi* when expounding his four new principles. In *Evangelii Gaudium*, at the beginning of his chapter on the social dimension of evangelization, Francis quotes Paul's statement in *Evangelii Nuntiandi*, no. 17 that "any partial or fragmentary definition which attempts to render the reality of evangelization in all its richness, complexity and dynamism does so only at the risk of impoverishing it and even of distorting it" (no. 176). Francis continues: "The kerygma has a clear social content: at the very heart of the Gospel is life in community and engagement with others" (no. 177).

---

[11] Scannone, "Pope Francis and the Theology of the People," 123.
[12] Ivereigh, *The Great Reformer*, 143.

Here the social magisterium of Francis represents a shift in mode from proclaiming the principles of Catholic social teaching to forming citizens in the principles of Catholic social praxis, just as *Populorum Progressio* represented a shift in the mode of Catholic Social Teaching toward integral human development on an international scale. Taking for granted Catholic Social Teaching as a theory, Francis develops it into a praxis with his four new principles (*Evangelii Gaudium*, no. 217-237): time is greater than space, realities are greater than ideas, unity prevails over conflict, and the whole is greater than the part. These are exhortatory and practical maxims, yet ones that Francis claims are "derived" from the four doctrinal-theoretical "pillars" of Catholic Social Teaching (*Evangelii Gaudium*, no. 221). These are a vision of how Catholic Social Teaching is supposed to be lived as a mode or practice in society through dialogue and encounter, beyond being a theoretical doctrine about the nature of society. In this way, Francis wishes his contribution to Catholic Social Teaching to be an orientation to praxis.

In conversation with this general environment in the universal Church and the Latin American Church, and in the process of his own leadership journey, Bergoglio began to enunciate these new principles. He applied them both *ad intra* and *ad extra*, within both ecclesial and social contexts. One encounters them in Bergoglio's aforementioned talks as Jesuit provincial in 1974 and 1980,[13] in various homilies and spiritual writings,[14] and in his 1999 and 2002 *Te Deum* homilies. The latter, held on "Argentina's national day," Bergoglio "turn[ed] ... into a chance to challenge and teach political leaders on behalf of the *pueblo.*"[15] It should accordingly surprise no one that Bergoglio continued to use these principles after he became Francis. This is true whether Francis is considering the link between evangelization and social development in *Evangelii Gaudium* or giving a speech before government leaders of various countries about how to pursue the common good.

---

[13] For the appearance of three of the principles in the 1974 talk at Provincial Congregation 14 of the Jesuit Province of Argentina, see "Una institución que vive su carisma," while for the 1980 talk containing all four principles, see "Formación permanente y reconciliación," both in Jorge Mario Bergoglio, *Meditaciones para religiosos*, ed. Diego de Torres (Buenos Aires: San Miguel, 1982) and Ivereigh, *The Great Reformer*, 400, note 13.

[14] Jorge Mario Cardinal Bergoglio, *Open Mind, Faithful Heart: Reflections on Following Jesus*, trans. Joseph V. Owens, SJ (New York: Herder & Herder, 2013), 96-97 (reality is more important than ideas, unity overcomes conflict), 116-117 (time is greater than space), 178-180 (reality is more important than ideas), 217-220 (time is greater than space, unity overcomes conflict).

[15] Ivereigh, *The Great Reformer*, 247; For how the homilies utilized the four principles, see 249-51.

Francis anticipated the detailed treatment of *Evangelii Gaudium* with a very brief exposition of two of the principles in his first encyclical, *Lumen Fidei*. The fourth chapter of that encyclical, "God Prepares a City for Them," reflects on the relation between "faith and the common good" (see no. 50). That chapter contains brief observations on how faith touches upon social dialogue and care for creation, anticipating the more extensive treatments of those topics found in *Evangelii Gaudium* and *Laudato Si'*, respectively. Faith illumines social realities and relationships by revealing that God and his love among humans are the foundation of the lasting "city". In the light of faith's "encounter with God's primordial love ... love ... becomes *a path and praxis* leading to the fullness of love" (*Lumen Fidei*, no. 51, emphasis added). Francis turns to "building" language that will later reappear in *Evangelii Gaudium*: faith "helps us build our societies in such a way that they can journey towards a future of hope. ... The hands of faith are raised up to heaven, even as they go about building in charity a city based on relationships in which the love of God is laid as a foundation" (no. 51). In this context, Francis reflects upon forgiveness in society: "unity is superior to conflict; rather than avoiding conflict, we need to confront it in an effort to resolve and move beyond it, to make it a link in a chain, as part of a progress towards unity" (no. 55). Francis, speaking of the connection now between faith and hope, invokes another of his principles in no. 57: "Let us refuse to be robbed of hope, or to allow our hope to be dimmed by facile answers and solutions which block our progress, 'fragmenting' time and changing it into space. Space hardens processes, whereas time propels toward the future and encourages us to go forward in hope." Francis has a reason for invoking these two principles together, for he claims that they stem from the same root tension in society, as will be explained below.

These two mentions of the principles were simply the beginning. Francis' frequent use of all four principles indicates that they are important maxims for praxis and pastoral exhortation for him. His only other encyclical, *Laudato Si'*, appeals to each maxim: "realities are more important than ideas" (nos. 110, 201), "the whole is greater than the part" (no. 141), "time is greater than space" (no. 178), and "unity is greater than conflict" (no. 198). There are numerous other examples of Francis' use of these principles in speeches and allocutions.[16] To

---

[16] The following is a non-exhaustive list of allocutions that contain mention of one or more of the principles, usually accompanied by a corresponding citation of *Evangelii Gaudium*. "General Audience," 19 June 2013 (unity is greater than conflict); "Homily at Vespers on Solemnity of the Conversion of Saint Paul the Apostle," 25 January 2014 (unity is greater than conflict); "Address to Members of the 'Catholic Fraternity of Charismatic Covenant Communities and Fellowships,'" 31 October 2014 (the whole is greater than the part); "Address to Third Congress of Ecclesial Movements and New Communities," 22 November 2014 (unity is greater than con-

understand why they are clearly important to Francis necessitates turning to his extended presentation in *Evangelii Gaudium*.

EVANGELII GAUDIUM: FOUR NEW PRINCIPLES

Francis outlines his four principles in chapter four of *Evangelii
Gaudium*, which is devoted to the "social dimension of evangelization." Part three, the immediate context, concerns attaining the common good and peace in the "slow and arduous task" of "becoming a
people" (no. 220). The new principles are: "time is greater than space"
(nos. 222-225); "unity prevails over conflict" (nos. 226-230); "realities are more important than ideas" (nos. 231-233); and "the whole is
greater than the part" (nos. 234-237). They "derive from the pillars of
the Church's social doctrine" (no. 221), namely, the dignity of the human person, the common good, subsidiarity, and solidarity.[17] Lest the
pillars remain "mere generalities which challenge no one" (no. 182),
Francis proposes his new principles to guide the application of the pillars in constructing a peaceful society. In this way, he affirms in the
order of theory the priority of the pillars, for his new principles "derive" from them, but, in the order of practice, he affirms the priority
of process, dialogue, and encounter. The origins of Leo XIII's seminal
encyclical *Rerum Novarum* in the various experiences and activities
of nineteenth-century lay European "social Catholicism" and in the
Thomistic theorizing of Leo's theologians, show that this twofold priority has always been more or less operative in the Church's approach
to the social question.[18]

flict, realities are more important than ideas, the whole is greater than the part); "Address to the Council of Europe," 25 November 2014 (time is greater than space,
unity is greater than conflict); "Address to European Parliament," 25 November
2014 (realities are more important than ideas); "Address to Young People in Manila,
Philippines (Impromptu remarks)," 18 January 2015 (realities are more important
than ideas); "Address to United States Congress," 24 September 2015 (time is
greater than space); "Address to the General Assembly of the United Nations Organization," 25 September 2015 (time is greater than space, an allusion to realities more
important than ideas); "Acceptance Speech for Charlemagne Prize," 06 May 2016
(time is greater than space, the whole is greater than the part). See also, *Amoris lae-
titia*, 19 March 2016, note 3 and 261 (time is greater than space). Interestingly, Francis has referred twice to Europe as "a family of peoples," in the address to the European Parliament and in his acceptance of the Charlemagne Prize.
[17] Francis cites Pontifical Council for Justice and Peace, *Compendium of the Social
Doctrine of the Church* (Vatican: Libreria Editrice Vaticana, 2004), no. 161. The
Compendium identifies the four "pillars" in the prior paragraph: the dignity of the
human person, the common good, subsidiarity, and solidarity (160). The German
translator of *Evangelii Gaudium*, perhaps thinking this reference would be lost on
the reader, makes this explicit: "Diese leiten sich von den Grundpfeilern der kirchli-
chen Soziallehre (Menschenwürde, Gemeinwohl, Subsidiarität, Solidarität) her."
[18] Robert Talmy, *Aux sources du catholicisme social: l'école de la Tour du Pin*
(Tournai, Belgium: Desclée, 1961), *passim*; Joan L. Coffey, *Léon Harmel: Entrepreneur as Catholic Social Reformer* (University of Notre Dame Press, 2003), 101-

Francis' axioms respond to ineluctable "bipolar tensions" that arise in the life of any social body and which must be "managed and resolved" in order to "construct a common project in the life of a people."[19] Each axiom is meant, then, to lead individuals and the community through some tension to a hard-won synthesis, without collapsing the tension to one side or the other. Romano Guardini's thought is the origin of Francis' attention to this notion of the synthesis of inherent tensions. Guardini believed that "inherent oppositions ... produce the creative tensions in human life and thought."[20] Guardini's classic work in this regard is his 1925 habilitation, *Der Gegensatz.*[21] It was this work in particular that Francis—then Bergoglio—had intended to study during his abortive 1986 doctoral studies in Germany.[22] The basic idea is that a healthy synthesis of opposites in a living thing, including civil society or the Church, will not destroy or collapse the contrast into one side or another. Rather, by embracing the polarity, the organism comes most fully alive.

In addressing the challenge of inherent tensions and conflicts in social development, Francis fills a gap left by Paul VI's *Populorum Progressio*, which "can ultimately be criticized for failing to

---

144; Russell Hittinger, "Pope Leo XIII (1810-1903): Commentary," in *The Teachings of Modern Roman Catholicism on Law, Politics, and Human Nature*, ed. John Witte Jr. and Frank S. Alexander (New York: Columbia University Press, 2007), 41.
[19] Jorge Mario Cardinal Bergoglio, "Nosotros como ciudadanos, nosotros como pueblo" (homily at Conferencia del Sr. Arzobispo en la XIII Jornada Arquidiocesana de Pastoral Social, Buenos Aires, October 16th, 2010), www.arzbaires.org.ar/inicio/homilias/homilias2010.htm#XIII_Jornada_Arquidiocesana_de_Pastoral_Social. Here Bergoglio identifies three such tensions and groups the first two principles of time over space and unity over conflict with the first tension of fullness and limitation. The second tension of idea and reality correlates with that principle of reality's superiority, and the whole's greatness with respect to the part responds to the global/local tension. In this homily, Bergoglio claims that these principles guide a group of people through the struggle amidst the tension to becoming both citizens (a "logical" category) and a people (a "historico-mythical" category).
[20] Robert A. Krieg, "Romano Guardini's Theology of the Human Person," *Theological Studies* 59, no. 3 (1998): 468, note 42; See also, Scannone, "Pope Francis and the Theology of the People," 129, note 35; Hans Urs von Balthasar, *Romano Guardini: Reform from the Source* (San Francisco: Ignatius, 1995), 23-24.
[21] Romano Guardini, *Der Gegensatz, Second Edition* (Mainz: Matthias-Grünewald, 1955). Translations in this article are made from the French translation, *La polarité: Essai d'une philosophie du vivant concret*, trans. Jean Greisch and Françoise Todorovitch (Paris: Cerf, 2010).
[22] See Ivereigh, *The Great Reformer*, 198, who adds, "Guardini's discussion drew on the work of a nineteenth-century Tübingen theologian, Johann Adam Möhler, who argued that in the Church, contrasting points of view (*Gegensätze*) are fruitful and creative, but can become contradictions (*Widerspruch*) when they fall out of the unity of the whole and develop in opposition to the body. This was precisely the distinction drawn on by Yves Congar in his discussion of true and false reform in the Church that had so influenced Bergoglio."

acknowledge the role that conflict plays in social change."[23] The Latin American bishops, otherwise appreciative of *Populorum Progressio*, sought to remedy this gap. Francis accordingly seeks to complete the work of Paul VI on social progress—"building a people" in Francis' terms—by presenting practical principles that speak to tensions that arise naturally within a social body, within a people. Since the principles correlate with "constant tensions in every social reality," they "can guide the development of life in society and the building of a people where differences are harmonized within a shared pursuit" (*Evangelii Gaudium*, no. 221). Furthermore, since these practical principles are based on a theoretical understanding of the dynamisms inherent in the nature of a society composed of human persons, they "derive from the pillars of the Church's social doctrine" (no. 221).

The principle "time is greater than space" speaks to the tension between "fullness and limitation," between hoping for continued improvement along the future horizon ("time") and the tendency to hold onto already established privileges, powers, or institutional responses in the present moment ("spaces"). Francis writes that this axiom should lead us to prefer "initiating processes rather than possessing spaces" (no. 223). For "time governs spaces, illumines them and makes them links in a constantly expanding chain, with no possibility of return" (no. 223). This axiom depends on deeper theological concepts such as time and even sin, yet it is meant to push the practitioner of Catholic Social Teaching to act by initiating new processes with a patient eye toward the future, in accordance with the objective criteria for achieving true human flourishing. Francis identifies the concern to "[obtain] immediate results which yield easy, quick short-term political gains, but do not enhance human fullness" with "space" (no. 224). Easy political success or the "mere absence of violence" is not the measure of flourishing, especially since the tensions of social life can only be harmonized through struggle (nos. 218, 220).[24] In this matter, Francis quotes Guardini's *End of the Modern World*: "The only measure for properly evaluating an age is to ask to what extent it fosters the development and attainment of a full and authentically meaningful human existence, in accordance with the peculiar character and the capacities of that age."[25] Time's superiority to space is the maxim Francis most frequently uses when addressing legislative bodies such as the US Congress and the EU Parliament. Francis ties this maxim to evangelization by calling to mind "the parable of the weeds among the

---

[23] Deck, "Commentary," 306. Perhaps Francis also seeks to fill a gap left by Guardini, who "offered no explicit guidance on how Christians should promote the coming of God's kingdom by means of their work and sociopolitical activities" (Krieg, "Guardini's Theology of the Human Person," 474).

[24] See also Bergoglio, "Nosotros como ciudadanos, nosotros como pueblo."

[25] See Pope Francis, *Evangelii Gaudium*, no. 224, quoting *Das Ende der Neuzeit: Ein Versuch Zur Orientierung* (Würzburg: Werkbund-Verlag, 1965), 30-31.

wheat (cf. Mt 13:24-30)," making the point that evangelization must take the long-run picture and be patient with process (no. 225).

The principle "unity prevails over conflict," arises from the same tension between fullness and limitation.[26] The tensions that arise from the nature of any social body, combined with tensions resultant on the personal and structural sins that are present in every concrete society, produce conflict. Francis sees such conflict as an opportunity for advancement, so long as the parties to the conflict do not, on the one hand, deny or ignore the conflict or, on the other hand, "embrace [the conflict] in such a way that they become its prisoners" (no. 227).[27] Drawing on the same beatitude evoked by Medellín's document on peace ("Blessed are the peacemakers" [Mt 5:9]), Francis proposes that "unity is greater than conflict" in such a way that "it becomes possible to build communion amid disagreement" (no. 228). Yet only those "who are willing to go beyond the surface of the conflict and to see others in their deepest dignity" are capable of building peace. Guardini's thought on the synthesis of contraries echoes in Francis' words here (no. 228):

> Solidarity, in its deepest and most challenging sense, thus becomes a way of making history in a life setting where conflicts, tensions and oppositions can achieve a diversified and life-giving unity. This is not to opt for a kind of syncretism, or for the absorption of one into the other, but rather for a resolution on a higher plane that preserves in itself the valid potentialities of the contrary sides.[28]

The synthesis of polarities in social development will not destroy persons and groups, but develop their potentialities in a new, higher way.

The axiom "realities are greater than ideas" corresponds to the tension between the ideas of politicians and social theorists and the social realities in question. Instead, Francis teaches, "ideas are at the service of communication, understanding, and praxis" (no. 232). When ideas do not correspond to reality's true nature, they cannot inspire effective action. The disconnection between words and things leads to "formal nominalism" and "rhetoric," generating a political discourse that fails to move the people and foster the common good. What does inspire to action are "realities illumined by reason." What Francis deplores is the

---

[26] Bergoglio, "Nosotros como ciudadanos, nosotros como pueblo."

[27] Compare with Bergoglio, *Open Mind, Faithful Heart*, 97: "Maybe we get entangled in conflicts hoping for personal triumph or sectarian advantage, or, conversely, we avoid conflicts and play the role of simple referees of history. But when we avoid conflicts, we run the risk of treating everything with bland neutrality: all values are equalized, and the supreme goal becomes pluralistic coexistence at the expense of truth and justice."

[28] I have modified the English translation by reference to the Spanish and French.

tendency of political ideologies to hinder the pursuit of the common good by failing to account for the concrete, historical life of the people. This principle therefore "has to do with the incarnation of the Word and its being put into practice" (no. 233, modified). In evangelization, the tension to be overcome is between "expansionist apostolic plans" and "the painful, humble reality of our people."[29] The principle responds to this tension by linking "inculturat[ing] the Gospel" with "perform[ing] works of justice and charity" (no. 233).

Despite the seemingly trite title, the principle "the whole is greater than the part" is a practical implication of solidarity and subsidiarity: the development of a people must preserve the diversity among the individuals and groups who compose the social order. Francis' favorite image for this maxim is the globalism of the "polyhedron", a globalism that does not dissolve the unique culture of each people (no. 236). That model is opposed on the one hand to the conformist notion of the "sphere", wherein all points are equally distant from the center and thus all cultures become "abstract" and homogenized. On the other hand, the image challenges those who would otherwise turn into "a museum of local folklore" by ignoring "the beauty which God bestows beyond their borders" (no. 234). Proponents of agrarianism need not see a conflict between local and global concerns. Francis simply wishes each people to make decisions on the basis of the widest notion of the common good possible, the "global" common good, but without failing "to sink our roots deeper into the fertile soil and history of our native place" (no. 235). The application to evangelization is that the Gospel always unifies in a "totality or integrity"—both that a people receives the Gospel totally in all its expressions of religion and all its occupations, and that the Gospel reaches to all people and all aspects of humanity (no. 237).

The parallels to Guardini's treatment of social bonds in *Der Gegensatz* are remarkable. First is the idea that social polarities have a surplus of "opposing potentialities" that render them capable of organization into superior levels of social life.[30] Nevertheless, the achievement of higher forms of social life does not destroy the lower forms but places them in a new position of development. This relates both to unity overcoming conflict and the whole being greater than the parts. For example, Francis says, "Nor do people who wholeheartedly enter into the life of a community need to lose their individualism or hide their identity; instead, they receive new impulses to personal growth" (no. 235). Second, that polarities are a source of much social conflict, owing to an imbalance in the living dynamism of social bodies. Hence the danger of relying on spaces over processes, since the task of peace requires constant attention to the "rhythm" of the social body's diverse

---

[29] Bergoglio, *Open Mind, Faithful Heart*, 96.
[30] Guardini, *La polarité*, 125.

poles.[31] Third, there is in Francis an echo of Guardini's point that friendship in society is the primary factor in sustaining a people. Francis' maxims can be said to flow from friendship and sustain friendship in society; they are maxims of solidarity. For his part, Guardini said that

> The complex tissue of opposing relations only constitutes, in effect, the scaffolding ... of the interpersonal community properly so-called. The communal bond properly so-called effects itself from another center: personal devotion in love and fidelity. This devotion is entirely impregnated by the opposing relations that we have described, but it transcends them. If someone were simply to envision the communitarian problem in the optic of these relations, the interpersonal bond would disappear, immediately the relations between contrary attitudes which ensure society would be changed to the point of no longer sustaining the community with any confidence.[32]

Finally, in both Guardini and Francis there is the cry of the Christian soul that only in the revelation of God in Jesus Christ are tensions capable of higher synthesis in a global view that does not destroy the particular. Francis claims that the principle that unity prevails over conflict is "drawn from the Gospel" and "reminds us that Christ has made all things one in himself: heaven and earth, God and man, time and eternity, flesh and spirit, person and society." Hence "Christ 'is our peace' (Eph. 2:14)" (no. 229). In Christ, the unity brought about by his "Spirit can harmonize every diversity" and "overcomes every conflict by creating a new and promising synthesis" (no. 230). Guardini, while speaking more about the epistemological position of the observer seeking a vision of the world, nevertheless speaks of the possibility of a "vision of the world [which is] the gaze that God directs to the world, that is, the gaze of Christ. In faith, we meet Christ to adopt his perspective and to participate in his gaze, if, while believing, we contemplate the world with his gaze at it."[33] It is in Christ that one is capable of recognizing the potential harmony of the diverse contraries and polarities in life. This gaze generates a personal awareness of the possibility of development and synthesis where the world simply sees irreconcilable groups and dynamics.[34]

---

[31] Guardini, *La polarité*, 127.

[32] Guardini, *La polarité*, 129. Later Paul VI would meditate on the link between solidarity, dialogue, and integral development in *Populorum Progressio*, no. 73.

[33] Guardini, *La polarité*, 183. The theme of Christ's gaze illumining reality reemerges in Francis' *Laudato Si'*, nos. 96-100.

[34] Francis recently addressed the connection between harmonizing tensions and the grace of God and identified this harmonization with the work of the Society of Je-

CATHOLIC SOCIAL TEACHING AS A PRAXIS CONSTITUTIVE OF
BUILDING A PEOPLE FOR PEACE

Someone who understands Catholic Social Teaching as merely the
application to new social conditions of a set of timeless theoretical
principles, worked out in abstraction from social realities and practices, would wonder how there could be any new principles. Such a
view may even be proof-texted from magisterial documents (e.g. St.
John Paul II, *Sollicitudo rei Socialis*, no. 4). Perhaps this model con-
ceives of Catholic Social Teaching as a Word not "already made flesh"
in social realities (cf. *Evangelii Gaudium*, no. 233). Instead, Francis
assumes that social doctrine is always being worked out in conversation with social realities and, thus, is capable of further elaboration and
development. The difference between older manuals of social doctrine
and what Francis is saying is clear upon comparison. Take, for example, the excellent manuals of Messner and Höffner.[35] These give un-
surpassed scientific presentations of social ethics based on a Catholic
understanding of human nature as social in combination with expert
knowledge of political history and economic theory. Francis does not
wish to obviate such presentations in his own principles but rather is
attempting to add something to them. Such manuals lack a treatment
of dialogue and do not give practical rules for working with others in
society to achieve the kind of social flourishing described in their manuals. Francis is therefore making explicit with his new principles what
has been implicit in the prior teaching and activities of the Church:
Catholic Social Teaching is not only a theory about the nature of society but also an ecclesially-embodied practice that seeks to achieve social peace. We might say that Francis' new principles reveal that Catholic Social Teaching is a practice that 1) has an intrinsic relation to the
end described by the theory, a just and peaceful society; and 2) thus
has, to use Alasdair MacIntyre's language, goods internal to its mode
of applying the theoretical principles to social realities beyond mere

___

sus. See Pope Francis, "Discourse to General Congregation 36 of the Society of Jesus, October 24, 2016," press.vatican.va/content/salastampa/en/bollettino/pub-
blico/2016/10/24/161024a.html: "this conceptual framework combining tensions
[found in the Formula of Ignatius]—the salvation and perfection of one's own soul,
and the salvation and perfection of one's neighbor's—from the higher realm of
Grace—is proper to the Society of Jesus. The harmonization of this and of all the
other tensions (contemplation and action, faith and justice, charism and institution,
community and mission…) is not expressed in abstract formulations but is achieved
in the course of time through what Faber called 'our way of proceeding'."
[35] Johannes Messner, *Social Ethics: Natural Law in the Western World, Second Edition*, trans. J. J. Doherty (St. Louis: Herder, 1965); Joseph Cardinal Höffner, *Christian Social Teaching, Second Edition*, trans. Stephen Wentworth-Arndt and Gerald
Finan (Cologne: Ordo Socialis, 1997). Messner had doctorates in theology, law, economics, and political and social theory, while Cardinal Höffner had written disserta-
tions in theology and economics.

expediency to that end.[36] Dialogue is not only the path to but also part of peace. The further implication of Francis' new principles is that the object of Catholic Social Teaching's theoretical knowledge, a peaceful and just society, can only be achieved by cultivating a "peaceful and multifaceted culture of encounter" (*Evangelii Gaudium*, no. 220) through an improved practice of Catholic Social Teaching in harmony with others in society. Hence "building a people ... is an ongoing process in which every new generation must take part" (no. 220).[37] Francis' new principles thus do not dispose of prior magisterial social doctrines but highlight that these are applied always in dialogue with others in the ongoing project of social development.

The orientation of these principles to action implies that applying the theory of Catholic Social Teaching to social realities is itself a practice normed by Catholic Social Teaching's own moral-social vision about what conduces to human flourishing. Just as the moral virtues are necessary means to and so constitutive of happiness, so, by analogy, the practice of Catholic Social Teaching is a means intrinsically related to achieving the just society as described by its theoretical principles. Therefore, Catholic Social Teaching as a praxis is partly constitutive of a just, peaceful society. A correct process of application constitutes a part of the peaceful society insofar as the application requires active dialogue with others in the midst of social tension. The process of dialogue, undergirded by Francis' four maxims, is a necessary means to social peace. Further, since peace requires harmonization of the members of a social body, peace in dialogue itself anticipates the social peace to be achieved as the end of dialogue. That dialogue is inchoate peace is all the more apparent once one remembers that every social unity is a unity of operation and is never a "space" definitively conquered or established.[38] In this way, the end described by Catholic Social Teaching is contained in it as a praxis and the praxis in the end. Hence Francis says that "these four specific principles ... can guide the development of life in society and the building of a people where differences are harmonized within a shared pursuit. I [offer them] out of the conviction that their application can be a genuine path to peace within each nation and in the entire world" (*Evangelii Gaudium*, no. 221). The process of Catholic Social Teaching, namely the four principles guiding members of a people toward a culture of

---

[36] For the concept of internal goods, see Alasdair MacIntyre, *After Virtue, Third Edition* (Notre Dame, IN: University of Notre Dame Press, 2007), 187-191.

[37] On the constant flux of social bodies on account of their inner contrarieties, see Guardini, *La polarité*, 128. For example, Guardini stresses the need for dialogue and balance between the tradition-innovation and communal-individual dynamics in any social group.

[38] Hittinger, "Coherence of the Four Basic Principles," 81.

encounter through dialogue, is constitutive of the goal of Catholic Social Teaching, a peaceful and just social life leading to the development of every person and the whole person.[39]

Take the example of "unity prevails over conflict." Two parties
opposed to one another in society could either ignore their conflict or
they could become "prisoners" to it (nos. 226-27). But if those parties
come together to dialogue about their conflict, they have already in an
incipient way achieved the goal of unity. The practice of dialogue is
therefore not an efficient and disposable means to unity and then to
peace, but it is the necessary means to it. A successful dialogue is similar to society, which is nothing other than a cooperative peace, an operational unity of many different persons, families, and communities.[40] The participant members of society lose something when they
are in general forced into unity, rather than overcoming conflict in cooperation with one another under authority. Pope Francis' contribution, therefore, is to discuss explicitly how Catholic Social Teaching
is a social theory that should both generate and be generated from a
way of life oriented as a necessary means to perfecting the discipline's
subject matter, society. As a praxis, it necessarily involves various
"encounters" or dialogues between government and people, scientists
and ethics, proposals and realities, one religion and another, and so on.
Should we expect anything different from a pope whose personal style
is best summed up in the phrase, "culture of encounter"?

The difficulty of such dialogue in a social body requires that the
practitioners of the dialogue be mentally capacitated for the task.[41]
Members of a people in dialogue with one another need each other's
differences, and yet the temptation is always present to either be overwhelmed by difference or attempt to annihilate it for the sake of unity.
Francis offers his principles as practical-hortatory axioms for this task
of dialogue. We might say that Francis is proposing maxims for solidarity, if we define solidarity with St. John Paul II as "a firm and per-
severing determination to commit oneself to the common good" (*Sollicitudo rei socialis*, no. 38; cf. *Evangelii Gaudium*, no. 228). Or again,

---

[39] An analogous example in *Evangelii Gaudium* of a means being constitutive of the
end is the place of ecumenism within the praxis of evangelization (no. 246). Divisions between Christians hinders the evangelization of people who have not received
the Gospel of Jesus Christ. Ecumenism ("commitment to [Christian] unity") must
now, by function of the concrete division between Christians, "no longer be a matter
of mere diplomacy or forced compliance, but rather an indispensable path to evangelization." This is especially true in "countries ravaged by violence," for Christians
are called to be a "leaven of peace."

[40] This is not to deny that authority is necessary for society to flourish. See Yves R.
Simon, *Philosophy of Democratic Government* (Indiana: University of Notre Dame
Press, 1993), 19-35.

[41] See Francis, *Evangelii Gaudium*, no. 205: "I ask God to give us more politicians
capable of sincere and effective dialogue aimed at healing the deepest roots—and
not simply the appearances—of evils in our world!"

Francis' maxims could be the Catholic Social Teaching equivalent of the rules laid down by St. Ignatius of Loyola at the end of the *Spiritual Exercises* for "having the right attitude of mind in the Church militant."[42] In both cases, the rules are affective helps to having the right kind of conduct toward a certain goal and to avoiding behavioral pitfalls toward the same goal. For example, Ignatius proposed to praise frequent confession to a priest and reception of Holy Communion (rule two), to praise the relics of the saints (rule three), and to not have the custom of speaking of predestination, or at least not in such a way as to mislead people (rule fifteen). These maxims are more about having the right affective and practical dispositions for the sake of thinking with the Church. Francis' are about having the right affective and practical dispositions for the sake of a people's social-political development. Both are ordered to conversion and growth, though Francis' are more explicitly social and aiming at integral development in both evangelization and "building a people."

CONCLUSION

Paul VI initiated a new line of Catholic Social Teaching with his decision to issue a social encyclical off the anniversary schedule of Leo's *Rerum Novarum*. With *Populorum Progressio*, Paul turns the discussion to integral human development and the place of the Church in progress in the modern world. The various local and universal teaching documents of the bishops that responded to *Populorum Progressio* advanced this discussion by focusing on the link between evangelization and social justice. Under the additional influence of Argentina's particular brand of liberation theology, Francis added the element of developing a people through its culture. Now Francis has offered his own contribution centered on his four new principles, systematically explained in *Evangelii Gaudium* but applied throughout his magisterial works. The contention here is that Francis is building upon the four great theoretical principles of Catholic Social Teaching (dignity, common good, solidarity, subsidiarity) by adding four new criteria for praxis (time is greater than space, unity overcomes conflict, reality is greater than ideas, and the whole is greater than the part). In his own way, Francis is attending to the interpersonal mode or method of Catholic Social Teaching as simultaneously being normed by the theoretical content and being constitutive of the social peace and integral development that Catholic Social Teaching identifies as the *telos* of the people.

That Francis intends to clarify how Catholic Social Teaching is to be practiced is clear enough. It is also clear that Francis means to apply his principles within the Church as much as without. This is evident

---

[42] St. Ignatius of Loyola, *The Spiritual Exercises*, trans. Anthony Mottola (New York: Image, 1964), 139-142. I am indebted to Russell Hittinger for this suggestion.

in Francis' political strategy within the Church as he "initiates processes" and lets go of what he considers "spaces." His mindset can be seen in his plan for the recent synods on the family, the modification of canon law in *Mitis Iudex Dominus Iesus*, the re-balancing of the weight of papal primacy and the authority of regional bishops' conferences, and in his appointment of bishops. Francis sees himself as holding tensions together in a process of development where others see contradictions or warring pairs of opposites. That Francis is turning Catholic Social Teaching into a praxis, however, does not prevent the conceptual content of his proposal from being at times vague. His new principles are meant to train one for dialogue through the formation of the imagination, as the principles are articulated in an imagistic way (e.g., the "polyhedron"). Perhaps this is to be expected from a Jesuit, whose tradition of formation in discernment has utilized pictures and plays to expand and hone the mindset of future leaders and missionaries. Yet inspiring images cannot substitute for knowledge about social bodies nor can they issue true judgments about particular questions. This must be why Francis emphasizes the "derivative" nature of the practical maxims as flowing from the four pillars. So long as Catholics do not mistakenly cast aside the theory of Catholic Social Teaching in seeking to better understand what dispositional attitude is necessary for practicing it, they will be able to appropriate constructively Francis' new contribution. To aim for short term successes by casting aside the teaching of prior popes, however, would be to hold on to the position of a party, and thus to deny that "time is greater than space" by clutching a "space" that prevents authentic development in the Church and the world.[43] ◼

---

[43] The author wishes to express his gratitude to the two anonymous reviewers, whose comments helped him to improve this article.

Contributors

Kevin Glauber Ahern, PhD is an assistant professor of religious studies at Manhattan College where he directs Peace Studies program. He has edited several books including *The Radical Bible, Visions of Hope: Emerging Theologians and the Future of the Church* and *Public Theology and the Global Common Good: The Contribution of David Hollenbach.* He is the author of *Structures of Grace: Catholic Organizations Serving the Global Common Good* (Orbis: 2015). @kevin_ahern

Raymond Olusesan Aina is a lecturer at the National Missionary Seminary of St Paul, Abuja, Nigeria. A moral theologian by training, his research interests include restorative peacebuilding, methodological issues in African thought, and contemporary issues in ethics. He is president of the Catholic Theological Association of Nigeria.

Marianne Tierney FitzGerald received her Ph.D. in Theological Ethics from Boston College and M.Div. from Harvard Divinity School. She currently serves as an administrator at the University of Notre Dame in the Office of Mission Engagement and Church Affairs and also teaches at Holy Cross College in Notre Dame, IN. Her research has focused on the connections between theology and women's activism, and she has previously published in Asian Horizons - Dharmaram Journal of Theology and *Commonweal* magazine.

Mari Rapela Heidt is an independent scholar whose research has focused on economic ethics, globalization, and the intersection of health care ethics and Catholic Social Teaching. She is the author of two textbooks, *A Guide to Writing About Theology and Religion* and *Moral Traditions, An Introduction to World Religious Ethics.* Her most recent book, *From Paul to Francis, Populorum Progressio and Economic Ethics,* is forthcoming.

Stan Chu Ilo is a research professor at the Center for World Catholicism and Intercultural Theology, at DePaul University, Chicago, USA where he coordinates the African Catholicism Project.

He is the Series Editor of African Christian Studies Series, Pickwick Books and the author of *The Church and Development in Africa*. His forthcoming book is titled, *A Poor and Merciful Church: The Illuminative Ecclesiology of Pope Francis in the African Social Context*.

Clemens Sedmak holds the F.C. Maurice Chair for Moral and Social Theology at King's College London and serves as FM. Schmoelz OP Visiting Professor at the University of Salzburg where he also directs the Center for Ethics and Poverty Research; he is currently Visiting Professor at the Center for Social Concerns and the Keough School of Global Affairs at the University of Notre Dame, Indiana. His most recent book "Church of the Poor" was published with Orbis in December 2016.

Matthew A. Shadle is Associate Professor of Theology and Religious Studies at Marymount University in Arlington, Virginia. He has published *The Origins of War: A Catholic Perspective* (Georgetown, 2011). His work focuses on the development of Catholic social teaching and its intersection with both fundamental moral theology and the social sciences, with special focus on war and peace, the economy, and immigration.

Barrett Turner is Assistant Professor of Theology at Mount St. Mary's University, Emmitsburg, MD. He earned his doctorate in Moral Theology/Ethics from the Catholic University of America in 2015, writing on the development of the Church's doctrine on religious liberty. His interests include fundamental moral theology, the development of moral and social doctrine, and political theology.

The Center for Bioethics & Human Dignity presents
THE 24ᵀᴴ ANNUAL SUMMER CONFERENCE

GENETIC & REPRODUCTIVE TECHNOLOGIES

Register by April 1ˢᵗ for early bird pricing

JUNE 22–24, 2017

on the campus of
TRINITY INTERNATIONAL UNIVERSITY
DEERFIELD, IL USA

PLENARY SPEAKERS

Marie T. Hilliard
National Catholic Bioethics Center

J. Benjamin Hurlbut
Arizona State University

Calum MacKellar
Scottish Council on Human Bioethics

C. Ben Mitchell
Union University

David A. Prentice
Charlotte Lozier Institute

Scott B. Rae
Talbot School of Theology

Gayle E. Woloschak
Northwestern University

Genetic & Reproductive Technologies Conference:
Join us as we explore current genetic and reproductive technologies with consideration of the ethical and theological implications for our individual and common humanity.

REGISTER

www.cbhd.org/conf2017

THE CENTER FOR
BIOETHICS & HUMAN DIGNITY
TRINITY INTERNATIONAL UNIVERSITY

In Partnership with:

AMERICANS UNITED FOR LIFE

Christian Medical & Dental Associations

Articles available to view
or download at:

www.msmary.edu/jmt

The

Journal of Moral Theology

is proudly sponsored by the

Fr. James M. Forker Professorship
of Catholic Social Teaching

and the

College of Liberal Arts

at

Mount St. Mary's University

MOUNT ST. MARY'S UNIVERSITY

College of Liberal Arts